SPIRITUAL
CPR

TODD PHILLIPS

Building the New Generation of Believers

COOK COMMUNICATIONS MINISTRIES
Colorado Springs, Colorado • Paris, Ontario
KINGSWAY COMMUNICATIONS LTD
Eastbourne, England

NexGen® is an imprint of
Cook Communications Ministries, Colorado Springs, CO 80918
Cook Communications, Paris, Ontario
Kingsway Communications Ltd, Eastbourne, England

First published in 2003 by:
TODDPHILLIPS.NET
46 Courtside Circle
San Antonio, Texas 78216

First NexGen Printing, 2005
Printed in the United States of America
1 2 3 4 5 6 7 8 9 10 Printing/Year 09 08 07 06 05

Cover Designer: Happy Day Design/Ray Moore
Cover Photo: PhotoSpin

Library of Congress Cataloging-in-Publication Data

Phillips, Todd, 1969-
  Spiritual CPR / by Todd Phillips.
     p. cm.
  ISBN 0-7814-4203-6 (pbk.)
  1. Witness bearing (Christianity) I. Title.
  BV4520.P48 2005
  248'.5--dc22

                              2004027329

To my angel on this earth, my wife, Julie,
and to our three children: Parker, Katherine, and Raney

TABLE *of* CONTENTS

ACKNOWLEDGMENTS

The completion of this book is a paramount event in my life for many reasons. For one, this book is the first of many I hope to complete in the area of Christian inspiration/Christian living. The greatest reason, though, is that I have seen what a group of dedicated people can do when they are free to fully explore and use the gifts given to them by God. With humility and deep respect I must acknowledge *God* who has proven to me time and time again that he is involved in the most intricate and private details of our lives and that he is a God of unparalleled intimacy and love.

The process of creating and refining this work rested on the shoulders of many loving and committed friends and family. My mother, *Patricia Smith*, volunteered her time and energy in editing the rough draft of this book so that it would not be a complete embarrassment. *Jimmy Myers* contributed to the Reader's Guide for this book. Jimmy has written professionally for Lifeway Christian Resources as well as authoring the youth edition of *Search For Significance*. Jimmy's talents are noteworthy and for him to devote his time, energy, and skills to this venture is truly humbling.

Those who have encouraged me to pursue writing professionally include the many thousands of people at events across this country who have encouraged me to consider penning my thoughts. Specifically, I thank the following people: Rich Hurst, Chris Eaton, Mark Wolf, Chuck Dishinger, Barney Randol, Dick Smith (step-father), Tom Phillips (father), Will Duke, Stephen Harpold, Greg Richards, John Berryhill, Jeff Harris, and Dana and Barbara Kirk.

I want to also acknowledge a few people who dove into the misery and uncertainty of my early days as a follower of Christ. These were the people who helped me to understand that I was truly a new creation in Jesus Christ. They are: Todd Riddle, John Walters, Gary and Janan Grissom (in-laws), John Ogleton, Susan Vest Stivers, Todd Praether, Kam Kronenburg, Joan Beal, Dan Woodall, Roger Dyer, Steve Stroupe, Greg Berry, Aldie Warnock, and the staff of Hyde Park Baptist in 1994 including: Dr. Ralph Smith, Dr. Mike Tignor, Rev. Joe Carrell, Bill McGinnis, and Chad McMillan as well as all the youth workers at Hyde Park from 1994 to the present.

Two people who have inspired this pursuit by their own accomplishments in writing and in life are *David Edwards* and *Max Lucado*. Max has been gracious enough to write the foreword for the book and encourage me through this entire process both personally and professionally. I'm honored to call him friend.

FOREWORD

by Max Lucado

Todd Phillips the optometrist. He wants to correct our vision. Lifting our eyes up off the world at our feet, he calls us to see the world in need. No more myopic agendas driven by what I want. More God-centered decisions spawned by what God wants.

Todd Phillips the cardiologist. Digging deep with the scalpel of truth, dislodging the sediments of self, invigorating a fresh flow of joy and gratitude.

Todd Phillips the expedition leader. Bidding all who dare board his ship to explore the rarely charted waters of faith living and faith giving. My friend Todd wears many hats in this book. If you're open to fresh vision, stronger heart, and a greater adventure—then you are holding the right book.

—*MAX LUCADO*

INTRODUCTION

Many believers at some point in their Christian experience will ask, "Why should I share my faith?" The answer may take different forms but the message is always the same: In Matthew 28:19–20, Jesus tells his followers to *make disciples* of all nations! The command to make disciples was not just for the eleven disciples on the hilltop that day but it is a command for every person today who calls himself a Christian! So, we share our faith because Jesus told us to, and that should be enough. The problem is ... it's *not* enough.

Why is God's command alone not enough to rally the church to a single-minded devotion to all activities related to the dissemination of the Gospel? Answer—no one likes to do anything without *reason!* My son, Parker, at the age of four, wants to know the reason for everything. From observations of nature to parental commands his mantra remains the same—"why?" "Why do birds fly? ... Why does the key start the car? ... Why can't I go potty outside like Gaby (our dog) does? ... Why do I have to go to bed now?" By the way, it's good to ask questions ... questions to our parents, to our bosses, especially to God.

Yet the prevailing attitude among believers is that we can answer any question about God or the human condition by saying, "The Bible says it so do it." This answer has never and will never satisfy the masses, pagan or believer. Yet, we persist in the notion that the community of faith will submit to the unreasoned (in their minds and hearts) commands of God, that they will bow to the sermon from the pulpit that insists we must, if we are truly followers of Jesus, follow the commands of God blindly. After all, how can one possibly be a member of the community of faith and not adhere to God's commands?

I further believe that those in the church who say they are motivated by the Great Commission solely for the fact that it is a command of God, and who further say they need no *reason* from which to act are in large part being dishonest to themselves, to others or both. I can say this so emphatically for one simple reason—the human condition, as proven by the biblical account of man's relationship with God, is for man to question God. Therefore, if a believer takes action in response to God's command without having an intrinsic understanding of the reason for the command, I submit that the person's fear of God, respect for God or deep understanding of the sovereignty of God act for them *as the reason* they obey God. Nonetheless, they have *reasoned* through the issue. We all must have a reason.

My contention then, and this will serve as the foundation for the first half of this book, is that *the church in our time has failed to give itself a sufficient reason to share the Gospel with the unbelieving world.* The passage in Matthew 28, known by many Christians as the Great Commission, is not enough to engage the church in the very battle for the lost world that the passage itself resolutely commands. Christians are not talking to their coworkers, family members and enemies about the claims of Jesus in the Bible. The church as a whole is not telling the story of Jesus on the cross, in the tomb, raised from the dead and alive today. The church is not engaging culture in sufficient terms to bring this great commission to fruition. Why not? Because we don't have *the reason.*

Many reasons have been offered up to the community of faith but no reason has compelled the community to *go*. No reason yet has given the believer any alternative but to *proclaim.* Reasons have pierced the hearts of many, pierced the wallets of many, pierced the pens of many ... but no reason has yet pierced the feet of the masses that sit in the pews.

I acknowledge and stand in awe at the otherworldly thrust of Christianity into nearly every corner of the earth. I am witness in my own environment of great acts of corporate and individual evangelism in our time. I am humbled at the global scale of our Christian faith and its ability to save for itself a remnant even in the darkest times of Christian history. I further acknowledge the sovereignty of God in this equation and find peace in the knowledge that he is in control in the midst of what I deem to be an evangelistic crisis on a global scale. Yet I believe that the church today is caught between joy-filled reflection on the history of Christianity's success and a collective stupor brought on by the radical and illogical shift in culture over the last forty years.

This evangelistic bewilderment has become the proverbial pink elephant in the cathedral of Christendom. Just as an overweight man might continue to eat fattening food, so does the church continue to respond to its illness by developing programs that have proven to be largely ineffective at either evangelizing the world or discipling believers. In our programmatic confusion, we are in effect feeding our illness the very food that makes it thrive. In our exploration of what our illness is we will come to terms with why we should want to cure it.

The second half of this book moves from the *why* of evangelism to the *how* of evangelism. This section, though, will not boil witnessing down to a four-point plan or a key question approach. Rather, I will peel back the layers of biblical teaching to discover what the relational aspects of witnessing are in Scripture and how we can apply those principles effectively and practically in our relationships with nonbelievers today. Also, if I am to accomplish my task of encouraging and empowering you to share your faith, then I must address the question, "What is the Good News?" So, much of the *how* section will address the *what*. How do we share our faith effectively? By knowing clearly what our message is! My fear has been that not only do the people of God not know why God has invited them to be part of his redemptive process but that the people of God are unclear as to the message they are to proclaim. Ironically, many Christians would be quick to tell you what they believe the "Good News" is. Many would also be able to give a quick answer to the question, "What is evangelism?" We will go beyond the answer, "Evangelism is sharing the Good News." We will find the church's missing link in experiencing a truly joyous life—knowing and sharing the true meaning of the Gospel.

I will use my personal testimony as a platform for explaining much of the "how" section of this book. I use my story not because it is unique or more eventful than any other, but simply because it is my experience and, therefore, the best source for me to draw from to provide you examples of the principles I discuss in this book.

For those who have found a way to integrate most tenets of the Christian faith into their everyday lives, but have been unable to successfully incorporate witnessing into their daily Christian experience, I want to encourage you. Read the following story from the book of Mark of a desperate father who brought his sick son to Jesus:

> Jesus asked the boy's father, "How long has he been like this?" "From childhood," he answered. "It has often thrown him into fire or water to kill him. But if you can do anything, take pity on us and help us." "'If you can'?" said Jesus. "Everything is possible for him who believes."

Immediately the boy's father exclaimed, "I do believe;
help me overcome my unbelief!" (Mark 9:21–24)

What does this passage have to do with integrating evangelism into our daily journey with God? Simple. Most of us lack
the desire to share our faith. Most of us do not possess an evangelistic zeal, but we do have passion for Bible study, worship
and service. Yet, if asked, most of us do want to have the desire
to share our faith. This desire for desire mirrors the confession
of the father in the above story who exclaims, "I do believe; help
me overcome my unbelief!"

This father was desperate to believe. He was desperate to do
anything he was required to do to save his son. In this moment
of desperation all bets were off and the only option was confession; confession that he did not believe and an impassioned
request for Jesus himself to give this desperate father the very
belief he needed to possess.

Do you lack a passion for sharing your faith? Are you desperate to experience the abundant life and complete joy God
promises every believer? If so, ask God for the passion you lack!

I believe God will use this book to help you discover the
hidden treasure of complete joy that comes from sharing your
faith! Remember what Jesus promised his disciples: "For where
your treasure is, there your heart will be also" (Matthew 6:21).

No matter why you now hold this book in your hands, be
prepared. Change—change in your heart for others, in your
mind about witnessing, in your soul as to your life's purpose
and in your actions as they relate to the misery of others—is
coming!

1
What's Your Cover?

I can't remember the sermon I preached. I can't remember what church it was. I seem to remember, though, ending the sermon that day with what Baptists call an invitation. I recall people coming down the aisles of the church but can't remember their faces. I can't even remember the name of the man who permanently altered my way of thinking. But I will never forget what he said.

He was standing at the back of the church leaning against the wall watching me. Listening. I could tell he was really listening. He was rather far away but I made a mental note, "He's African American, in his sixties, wearing some kind of uniform." When the church service was over I made my way up the main aisle to the front of the church where I had seen the man moments before and where my information table was. I wanted to thank him for—well, listening; but I couldn't find him, so I focused my attention on the people around my table and began to shake hands with some, pray with others. (I always bring resources and information about my ministry so people can learn more about my ministry and me.)

My ministry was, and still is, traveling and telling nonbelievers about Jesus and encouraging Christians to tell nonbelievers about Jesus. I felt, up to that point in my ministry, that I had a pretty clear picture of what evangelism was all about. I felt strongly that Christians needed to get out of their comfort zone and share Jesus with their friends, coworkers, family members and even their enemies. I knew my message was encouraging rather than accusing because people constantly offered up praises for my "fresh and inspiring" message. They would say, "I feel like calling my friend when I get home and telling him all about Jesus!" I knew, though, that something was missing. If the message I preached (which was the same type of message that pastors preach all over the country) was so inspiring then why did statistics show that over two-thirds of the people in church still didn't share their faith?

As the crowd dwindled I prepared to leave by putting all of my materials in a cardboard box. I was almost finished when I noticed someone out of the corner of my eye. There he was, the man I was looking for. He was casually pushing a mop and a bucket across the tile floor, a contemplative smile on his face. The wheels of the big yellow bucket full of milky brown water made a muffled clicking sound as they rolled over the indentations between the tiles on the floor. The uniform that I'd spied from the pulpit was a pair of grayish-blue overalls. His hair was streaked with gray and he hunched over the mop as he walked. "Son, that was a great message," he said in a soft, reassuring voice. "I like your passion for sharing Jesus with lost folks." I'd heard those words from others who were just as sincere, but his words drew me in.

"Well, uh, I appreciate those words of encouragement." I wasn't sure what else to say but I didn't want the man to leave so I asked, "How long have you been working at this church?"

"Thirty years."

"Thirty years!" I echoed.

"Thirty years," he said with a chuckle.

"Does your job ever get boring? You know, kind of monotonous?"

He wrinkled his brow as if he was confused, then his face brightened up as he looked around in all directions like he was about to tell me a big secret. He put one foot on the rim of the bucket, leaned over using the mop for support and whispered,

"My *job* isn't cleaning floors with this mop. My job all my life has been sharing Jesus with lost folks, like you were preaching about in the sermon. This mop and this bucket," he said, looking over both shoulders one more time, *"that's my cover."*

He let out a joyful giggle from deep down in his belly as he walked away, not knowing (or maybe he did) that he had just changed my life. He gave me the very piece, the something, I knew I was missing in my quest to empower the church to share Jesus with everyone—the 'why!' I left the church that day, my mind racing, pondering what the elderly man had said. "That's my cover!" Only three words, but they were the three words that would permanently alter my perspective on witnessing. What a claim to make as I look back on that moment, that three words changed my worldview. Three small words became my catalyst for change. I can look back throughout my life and describe people who have changed me by who they were, classes that have changed me by what I learned, books that have changed me by introducing me to new philosophies and ways of thinking—but I had never been changed so profoundly by a single statement. "That's it!" I thought to myself. "The church today has lost sight of its true assignment!"

Christians today are so weighed down by their job and family responsibilities that they can't imagine adding one more responsibility, one more obligation to the long list they already have. They see evangelism as another unwanted responsibility. They see evangelism as yet another thing to add to their grocery

list of "must do's." They cry out from their seats in church services all over the country. "Job, family, dry cleaners, bills, softball,
committee meeting, retirement planning and now witnessing—
it's too much!"

Adding to this sense of obligation, many believers are just
plain uncomfortable sharing their faith with anyone. Their cries
are not audible, but I can read it in their faces as I preach to
them. I can see it when they shift in their seats revealing their
discomfort at the idea of asking a coworker, "What will happen
to you when you die?" They squirm at the thought of sitting
down next to their agnostic uncle and pulling out a *Four Spiritual
Laws* pamphlet and reading each page as though it were a sales
pitch. The very word evangelism brings these kinds of thoughts
into people's minds.

Then that man walked up to me and with three words,
"that's my cover," he gave me a magnificent glimpse into what
could be. He showed me that the church is putting the cart
before the horse when it comes to evangelism. We're showing
Christians *how* to share their faith before we ever really tell
them *why* they should share their faith.

I remember my Uncle Kenneth telling me, "no one will ever
want to learn how to dig a hole unless you tell them why they're
digging. If you tell them they are digging a well to provide life-
giving water for their family, they will dig with enthusiasm, but
if you just tell them to dig, they'll drop the shovel and walk away.
The *why* is what motivates 'em." Uncle Kenneth was trying to
teach me that people must be taught the *why* so they will want
to learn the *how*. When the *why* becomes compelling enough,
then the *how* becomes a must!

The church, for centuries, has used Matthew 28:19–20, "Go
and make disciples ... baptize ... and teach ... " as the clarion call
of the church to tell the world about Jesus. Yet, it is statistically
proven that, for the vast majority of Christians, sharing our
faith because Jesus tells us to share isn't a good enough reason.
The pulpits have been filled for centuries with impassioned

preachers shouting the words from this passage and wondering why their parishioners were still not sharing their faith.

Christians as a community seem not to know the *why* of evangelism. They see evangelism as just digging another hole. They are not told that each thrust of the shovel digs deeper into a ground soaked with eternal water—an eternal well-spring of true life for the nonbeliever and a virtual fountain of youth for the believer who shares his or her faith.

Many (if not most) books I have been exposed to on evangelism or witnessing focus on a specific method or technique. Titles such as *Christians and Witnessing: Ten Basic Steps* (Campus Crusade), *Evangelism That Works* (Barna) and the classic, *The Master Plan of Evangelism* (Coleman), all tell us how to witness but don't adequately approach the subject of why we witness in the first place. Campus Crusade has the four-point approach to witnessing and the Baptists for many years mirrored the methods developed by Campus Crusade and called it the Four Spiritual Laws. Evangelism Explosion (E.E.) has expanded globally as a witnessing tool. Recently, there have been programs using a different spin on these witnessing concepts such as F.A.I.T.H. and L.I.F.E. These new paradigms teach the person who is witnessing to an

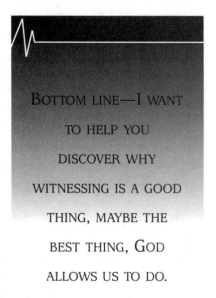

BOTTOM LINE—I WANT TO HELP YOU DISCOVER WHY WITNESSING IS A GOOD THING, MAYBE THE BEST THING, GOD ALLOWS US TO DO.

unbeliever to focus on showing them the beauty of eternal life rather than the threat of eternal damnation. All of these are valid, God-given techniques for sharing the Gospel. In fact, I have included a list of web sites and a recommended reading list on the subject of evangelism in the back of this book (appendix A).

Yet the issue is not finding a better method. Methods are only effective if they are *used*. People must *want* to share their faith for these methods to be of use. The problem lies in the lack of desire for some, fear for others. But I believe that for those who do not engage in the act of sharing their faith, whatever the reason, the root issue is a lack of wisdom.

I have heard it said that knowledge is the ingesting of information and that wisdom is applying that ingested information rightly to life's circumstances. Having the methodological knowledge for effective witnessing, if not coupled with the ability to apply that knowledge rightly to each of life's situations, will not result in godly fruit. In other words, knowing how to witness must be preceded by a reasoned *why*. Most believers know that we are to share our faith. This knowledge applied wrongly, though, results in the false belief that evangelism is merely an obligation. This same knowledge applied rightly results in the correct perception of evangelism as a marvelous opportunity.

My desire is to permanently free you from the bondage of wrongly perceiving evangelism as an obligation or burden for the rest of your life. I believe God will give you a fresh and supernatural passion for sharing your faith and then show you how to share it in a way that suits your God-given personality.

Bottom line—I want to help you discover why witnessing is a good thing, maybe the best thing, God allows us to do. Once I have convinced you of the lottery-winning opportunity God has given you, I will then show you how to dive into the hopelessness and misery of people, how to love them out of their spiritual ditch and into the kingdom of God. Finally, I will show you what rewards await you as you submit to God's plan for your life in the area of witnessing. You will come to understand how sharing your faith can be your very own spiritual fountain of youth bringing you back to a truly passionate existence with God.

2
The Terrible Twos

Do you remember back in junior high when you could get a date just by writing a note? The note would say, "Will you go steady with me?" Then there would be two boxes below the question with "yes" beside one and "no" beside the other. If you weren't sure that your future soul mate would say "yes," then there was a third box with the word "maybe" next to it. Would you give the note directly to the person you liked? Absolutely not! You would give the note to your friend so your friend could give it to another friend who would then give it to the person you liked. Most of us don't get dates that way any more because we're adults, and adults don't send notes like kids do because we have matured beyond such childish behavior. What is acceptable for a child is usually considered inappropriate for an adult—and rightly so.

In our everyday lives there are cultural milestones that mark our growth to adulthood. A baby moves from crawling to walking then to running. A child learns to talk and is potty trained. A young child's first day of school is a huge marker of maturity. From the first crush to high school graduation, parents and society expect a child to become a mature adult. To expect anything less than full maturity into adulthood is to damage the child and ultimately damage the society in which he or she lives.

Never-Never Land

I remember when I was a kid getting excited any time we went out to eat at our favorite Red Lobster, just down the street from our house in Austin, Texas. Although the food was great, it wasn't the fried shrimp that made the trip such a treat. No, my excitement was tied to something very different—the huge bowl of mints at the front door. They were free! Instead of being polite and getting one or two mints, I always dipped both hands into the bowl and walked out with sixty or seventy mints. Why? Because they were free! Such silliness can be overlooked when the culprit is a five year old, but what if a forty-year-old man stuffed the pockets of his sport coat with handfuls of mints?

I have a long-time friend who, like me, had the attitude as a child that getting something for nothing was the best thing in the whole world. To this day he has not let go of the idea of getting something for nothing. Instead of maturing beyond

> TO EXPECT ANYTHING LESS THAN FULL MATURITY INTO ADULTHOOD IS TO DAMAGE THE CHILD AND ULTIMATELY DAMAGE THE SOCIETY IN WHICH HE OR SHE LIVES.

that childish philosophy, he carried it into his adult life. Being extremely intelligent, he completed two degrees in college but continued to work at a video store even after he graduated. I asked him once why he kept working at such a dead-end job even though he had two degrees. I'll never forget his answer. He said, "I get free videos!"

Sadly, his life became a testimony to what happens if we don't grow up and let go of our childish attitudes. He got his paycheck every Friday, grabbed six or seven videos off the shelf at the store, cashed his paycheck, drove by the convenience store to pick up a twelve-pack of beer, then went home and laid down on the couch to start his "free movie marathon" as he called it. He was convinced the whole time that he was somehow beating the system.

With his education he could have landed a professional job that paid him five times what he was making at the video store, paid the money to rent ten movies a day every day and still come out ahead. He was blinded by a childish philosophy that had no place in his adult life.

We look at these people and feel sorry for them because they never reach maturity. We pity them because we know the responsibilities, blessings and opportunities that come from mature adulthood. Yet in the church today, many Christians are trapped in what I call the terrible twos of their Christian walk. They have taken the philosophies of their spiritual youth and brought them into their spiritual adulthood. Many of us are stunted in our spiritual growth and we think it's normal! The narrow and sometimes incorrect ideas and philosophies of our Christian infancy are the standard by which we measure ourselves. We look around and find church members who have been in the church for years still thinking and acting like spiritual toddlers and we're forced to conclude, tragically, that this must be what spiritual maturity is. The result is a generation of Christians who understand mature Christianity as a state of chronic frustration with little progress!

Crawling Into Obsolescence

Although we may be stunted in many areas of our spiritual maturity, the area that we will focus on is evangelism. Evangelism is a facet of our Christian walk where, more than in any other, the majority of us never move beyond a wobbly crawl. We remain babes moving only a few spiritual feet at a time. The greater and more detrimental issue, however, is that as we crawl around aimlessly in the area of evangelism, we look in all directions only to find "mature" Christians crawling with the same trepidation. Many churches today look like huge childcare facilities where even the elders of the church are crawling alongside the new Christian when it comes to evangelism. New believers look around and conclude that it is normal to crawl for decades; that it is normal to maintain the status quo and never strive to take a first step. Oh, they see a few people walking around the church, but those people are celebrated as different or unique or exceptional. The one or two in the church who developed the ability to actually run are now on foreign soil somewhere sharing the Gospel. Meanwhile, everybody who's still crawling says that those foreign missionaries were a little different anyway.

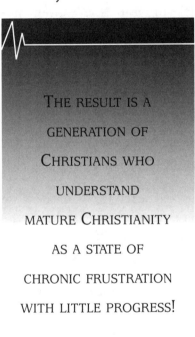

THE RESULT IS A GENERATION OF CHRISTIANS WHO UNDERSTAND MATURE CHRISTIANITY AS A STATE OF CHRONIC FRUSTRATION WITH LITTLE PROGRESS!

Those new Christians who are supposed to be crawling ask the other "more mature" Christians who are still crawling, "Why are all the members who have been in the church for years still crawling? Shouldn't we want to take steps?"

The long-time church member replies, "Yes, evangelism is a part of our maturing process. Jesus tells us in Matthew to make disciples, baptize and teach. When it comes right down to it we are supposed to witness to people. Evangelism is one of our obligations as a Christian. But very few people are comfortable with the idea of sharing their faith. So we've developed an annual event called 'spiritual emphasis week' or 'revival' where we all *have to* share our faith or at least help behind the scenes."

With that well-intentioned but misguided philosophy, the training has begun for the new believer. He or she begins to falsely surmise that evangelism is an obligation, a "have to" of his or her new walk with God. The idea starts to seep into his or her thoughts that sharing his or her faith is nothing more than a program or an event and is never meant to be a lifestyle. He or she looks at the environment around him or her and concludes that walking in the area of evangelism is too much effort after all—or more people would be struggling to get on their feet.

This process perpetuates itself through the generations of new Christians until the church becomes completely ineffective at fulfilling the clarion call of Christ to "go and make disciples of all nations, baptizing them in the name of the Father and of the Son and of the Holy Spirit, and teaching them to obey everything I have commanded you. And surely I am with you always, to the very end of the age" (Matthew 28:19–20).

As a result, our churches have become country clubs instead of the spiritual hospitals God designed them to be. We create concrete monstrosities complete with bookstores, workout facilities and even Christian schools where we can keep our clean Christian kids away from those dirty lost kids in the public schools. If we are careful and plan properly we never have to enter the "Land of the Lost" at all. We can effectively live our entire lives inside the modern-day convents we have created. Creating and maintaining Christian country clubs has become the goal of far too many congregations and this further breeds

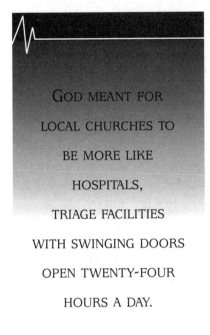

GOD MEANT FOR

LOCAL CHURCHES TO

BE MORE LIKE

HOSPITALS,

TRIAGE FACILITIES

WITH SWINGING DOORS

OPEN TWENTY-FOUR

HOURS A DAY.

the unbiblical notion that we are to separate from the unbelieving world (John 15–17).

Instead of turning outward, we turn inward. We choose to stick with our own and develop few if any relationships with unbelievers. Our worship services are often filled with believers who have inadvertently developed a convoluted sub-culture in word and deed, so that those who venture in from the outside world feel utterly disconnected to the goings-on around them.

God meant for local churches to be more like hospitals, triage facilities with swinging doors open twenty-four hours a day. Churches are to be staffed with well-educated, gifted, empathetic and impassioned people who are prepared for even the worst "patient" to come through the doors. Imagine someone rolling in on a spiritual gurney, a Christian friend pushing him into the facility desperate for his Christian family to help him heal his ill friend.

Most of us when we think of the church as a hospital agree that it should be that way, but the scenario breaks down when we are forced to consider where we fit into the picture: "Am I a surgeon or a secretary? An anesthesiologist or an ambulance driver?" If you are wondering, the answer to these questions is a simple "yes." We are all these people. Paul said, "I am all things to all people so that some might be saved" (see 1 Corinthians 9:22). For most of us, though, this is not the answer we want to hear. Most of us aren't comfortable with the idea of being anybody in the picture. Most of us say, "I'm not equipped nor do I desire to be an employee of either a real or a spiritual hospital."

Fair enough.

What's in It for You?

For those of us who have no desire to share our faith or who see evangelism as someone else's responsibility, let me suggest at this point that this "what's in it for me" perspective is an

THE WORLD SCREAMS FOR US TO TAKE ALL WE CAN GET, BUT GOD SOFTLY WHISPERS, "GIVE ALL YOU'VE GOT."

unfortunate but very real philosophy that has seeped into the church from the world. The world waves the banner in the face of every man, woman and child from birth that we must take all we can get. The world says, "You'd better grab what you can grab while you can grab it because there are no free lunches. No one else is going to look out for you so you need to look out for yourself." The world screams for us to take all we can get, but God softly whispers, "give all you've got." God constantly reminds us that our thoughts are not his thoughts; his actions are not our actions (see Isaiah 55:8). What the world offers us is a lie. What God offers is truth, and he promises the truth will set us free (see John 8:32).

We must get beyond the terrible twos when it comes to sharing our faith. Unfortunately, we are locked into pat answers and silly quips when we respond to the idea of sharing our faith. I hear things such as, "I have to share my faith. It's my obligation as a Christian." Comments like these are nothing less than spiritually childish thinking that has absolutely no place in the church today. When we let go of our childish thinking, statements such as "I have to share my faith," will be replaced with "I get to share my faith!" Instead of seeing evangelism as an obligation, the mature Christian will see evangelism as the greatest opportunity God has given man.

Paul made it clear in his letter to the church at Corinth when he wrote, "When I was a child, I talked like a child, I thought like a child, I reasoned like a child. When I became a man, I put childish ways behind me" (1 Corinthians 13:11). Paul acknowledged the very real and appropriate stage of spiritual infancy we must all go through, but he then speaks of the move to spiritual maturity as the natural progression of every believer. Just as children become adults, so do spiritual infants become mature.

3
Giving All You've Got

There is a tremendous sense of importance given to the last words of a dying man. You may have seen a movie that portrays this concept or you may have experienced this firsthand through the death of a loved one. Whether this truth has been dramatized for you on screen or you have personally experienced it, the result is the same. The scenario goes like this: An elderly man knows he is close to his last breath and calls his grandson into the room. As the grandson stands over his frail grandfather, the elderly man makes the effort to touch his grandson's leg. "Boy, I'm close to death now and I want you to do one thing for your grandfather."

"Sure, Grandpa. Anything."

"I want you to finish college and become the doctor I know you can be." Grandpa's hand goes limp and he lets out his dying breath.

What do you think the young man will do?

He's going to finish college and become a doctor! After all, it was the *last request of a dying man!* One can't help but consider that any man who has lived a long life would have many truths to share, many pearls of wisdom from which to choose. Yet, this man chose not to say, "I love you" or "Be nice to people." He gave his grandson the gift of guidance: "Finish college and become a doctor." Grandpa must have decided that there was no need for him to reiterate his love for his grandson because the young man already knew that his grandfather loved him dearly. He chose instead to call him out to be something great, to do something significant with his life.

Jesus did the same with his disciples on a mountain outside Galilee. His last words to his disciples would be spoken there. What he would say would not just change the lives of the eleven men, but would be the gunshot that would start a race that had, ironically, already been won, evidenced by Jesus standing in his resurrected and glorified body before them. He had broken the stronghold of sin and claimed victory over death for everyone who would believe in him.

The eleven disciples met him on that Galilean mountain as Jesus had instructed them. They must have been holding their breath in complete disbelief. Here was their master—ALIVE! He had appeared to them in the days before but some of them just couldn't wrap their minds around the reality that he was actually alive. They saw him die in agony on that cross, just weeks before. They witnessed his lifeless body pulled down from the cross, wrapped in grave clothes and laid in a tomb. He was dead, but now he stood before them very much alive. They were forced to accept that his appearance in the upper room was not an apparition or a dream—they knew that now.

So, why had he brought them to this place at this time? What would the Messiah say to them? Each reasoned in his heart that this must be a farewell, but what words would the Savior of the world choose to leave with them? What would a perfect God choose from all truth to share at a moment so paramount in time? He was, after all, the God of the universe. All truth for all time was embodied in this man standing before them. Perfection himself was about to speak perfect truth.

All authority in heaven and on earth has been given to me. Therefore go and make disciples of all nations, baptizing them in the name of the Father and of the Son and of the Holy Spirit, and teaching them to obey every-thing I have com-manded you. And surely I am with you always, to the very end of the age. ... You will receive power when the Holy Spirit comes on you; and you will be my wit-nesses in Jerusalem, and in all Judea and Samaria, and to the ends of the earth (Matthew 28:18–20; Acts 1:8).

ALL TRUTH FOR ALL TIME WAS EMBODIED IN THIS MAN STANDING BEFORE THEM. PERFECTION HIMSELF WAS ABOUT TO SPEAK PERFECT TRUTH.

With that he shot straight up into the air and soon a cloud hid him from their sight. If I had been there I would have thought to myself, "He didn't remind us to 'Love the Lord with all your heart' or 'Love your neighbor as yourself.' He said noth-ing about perfect church attendance. He gave no methodology, no format from which to work." He could have said any number of things for his last earthly words, but he chose to tell us to "make disciples ... baptize ... and teach." His disciples must have realized the uniqueness of these words Jesus spoke because they left from there and went on to give their entire lives making disciples, baptizing, and teaching.

I must mention here that the disciples did need a little friendly motivation to start conquering the world with the Good News. In Acts 1:10–11:

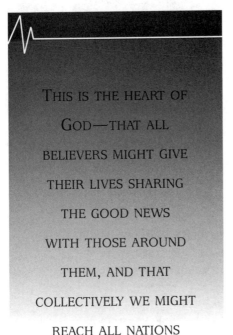

THIS IS THE HEART OF GOD—THAT ALL BELIEVERS MIGHT GIVE THEIR LIVES SHARING THE GOOD NEWS WITH THOSE AROUND THEM, AND THAT COLLECTIVELY WE MIGHT REACH ALL NATIONS WITH THE GOSPEL.

They were looking intently up into the sky as he was going, when suddenly two men dressed in white stood beside them. "Men of Galilee," they said, "why do you stand here looking into the sky? This same Jesus, who has been taken from you into heaven, will come back in the same way you have seen him go into heaven."

They were so awed by the sight of their Lord flying into the heavens that they had to be broken from their stupor by two angels. In essence, the angels were saying to the disciples, "Okay now. Move along. There's nothing more to see here." Yet the disciples were like rubberneckers at the scene of an accident on the highway who slow almost to a stop looking at the accident while they and sometimes thousands of others need to get on down the road. Can you imagine how many angels must be standing over the believers in church services all across this country and around the world demanding the answer to one question, "Why do you sit here?"

The church has lapsed into corporate inactivity when it comes to witnessing. Undoubtedly there are many believers who are fervently sharing their faith. Yet, in America today, the numbers simply do not lie. The vast majority of the American church is sitting in the pews with a "get from" instead of a "give to" mentality.

Consider one other glaring reality of this scene on that Galilean mountaintop. Jesus chose not to amass an army to spread his Gospel. He instead chose eleven ragtag young men from very different backgrounds and professions; men who at times could not get along with each other, let alone those around them; men who were not scholars or politicians or wealthy entrepreneurs; men who were not theologians or teachers. They were fishermen and tax collectors. They were a collection of men that no business owner or manager today would even consider allowing to work together in the most menial of jobs. Yet Jesus, the God-man, in his perfect wisdom, did choose these men. He chose them not to work in insignificant roles, which is what their resumes would demand. He instead chose them (the disciples) to be his tools to saturate the globe with the Gospel. He goes so far as to tell them where to start—in their hometown of Jerusalem. He then tells them where they will end the race—at the ends of the earth.

These last words from the mouth of Jesus were not only for those eleven disciples on the hill that day. These words are a call for everyone who claims Jesus as Lord, even today. This is the heart of God—that all believers might give their lives sharing the Good News with those around them, and that collectively we might reach all nations with the Gospel.

We attend churches today, some with 2,000 or more active members, and we cringe or simply laugh in disbelief that our large church could even begin to reach our entire city with the

Gospel. To even mention the idea that we might move beyond the walls of our city and propose to reach a neighboring town or another state is often dismissed as the idea of passionate but unrealistic believers. Yet, God himself gave charge to just those kinds of people—eleven young and passionate but unrealistic believers. Why did Jesus have so much confidence in only eleven men? How could he possibly lay out such a ridiculous goal—eleven men—the entire world? Yet they achieved exactly what he sent them to do. Where was his army? There they stood in all their tarnished splendor. What made them different? Answer—they *gave*! These eleven men did what very few since have chosen to do. They gave all that they were to Jesus. In that act of surrendering every scintilla of their being to Jesus, God was able to do more through them than he would through an army of thousands of fair-weather, half-committed Christian soldiers.

4
Total Devotion

I've heard this many times: "One person totally devoted to God can do infinitely more than a thousand people who have simply been awakened by God's spirit" (author unknown). This describes accurately what was transpiring on the mountain as Jesus spoke his last earthly words to his disciples. One totally devoted person can do more than a thousand people who have given their lives to Jesus but have yet to give their *lifestyles* to him. Jesus gave charge to eleven totally devoted men knowing that they would give more to his mission than if Jesus had amassed an army of 11,000 people who had accepted Jesus as their Savior but not accepted him as the Lord and Ruler of their lives.

Those who still try to control their own lives I call "pew potatoes." They are like Christian "couch potatoes." Pew potatoes come to church on Sunday, sit in the pews and wait for God to perform. For them, church is not about what they can give in worship to God but what they expect to get from God. They view God as the giver—the one who is expected to perform for the audience. I hear comments such as, "The pastor better preach a good sermon or I'm going to quit coming to the services." Others will remark, "If the music continues to get more contemporary and they keep taking out the old hymns, our family is out of this church and we're taking our tithe with us."

So they sit in their pews and critique the style of worship and the format of the sermon and the color of the carpet and, sadly, they miss entirely what truly should be happening. God is not to give a performance to satisfy our desires and preferences. God is not the performer on the stage. We are not the audience who judges and critiques. No. We are called to something radically different. We are called to come together as the body of Christ to give a performance for God! We are to worship in spirit and in truth to satisfy the desires of the heart of God. God is, in fact, the audience, and we are the performers. He is to lovingly critique our hearts and then reward us based on what our deeds truly deserve (Jeremiah 17:10). The sermon is not to warm our hearts but to break and mold our spirits. The worship is not to be critiqued by us based on style and tempo—rather, we are to be critiqued by God based on the authenticity of our worship to him. We have no right but the right to give ourselves completely to him. Our time in corporate worship is the training ground, the breeding ground for people who would give everything to God. *Give. Give! GIVE!* It is not about taking all you

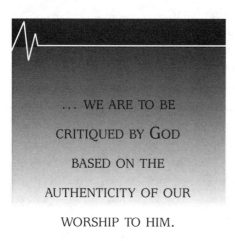

... WE ARE TO BE CRITIQUED BY GOD BASED ON THE AUTHENTICITY OF OUR WORSHIP TO HIM.

can get from the institution of the church. Rather, it's about giving all you've got to and for the person of Jesus. The disciples bit down on the meat of this truth like a pit bull and never let go.

In contrast, most of us have been led to believe that if we give our time and energy to someone, we have, in the process, spent what we perceive to be limited resources. If we spend time then we cannot get it back. If we spend our energy physically, emotionally, or spiritually, we become tired physically, emotionally, or spiritually. We look at our friends, coworkers, and family members who do not have a relationship with Jesus, and it tires us to even think of diving into their extremely dysfunctional lives and dealing with issues that we have spent years getting out of ourselves. We can't imagine God in his love for us possibly wanting us to spend what we perceive as our limited resources on people who are so beyond help.

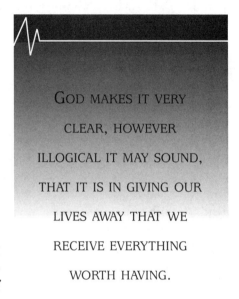

GOD MAKES IT VERY CLEAR, HOWEVER ILLOGICAL IT MAY SOUND, THAT IT IS IN GIVING OUR LIVES AWAY THAT WE RECEIVE EVERYTHING WORTH HAVING.

Then God gently shows us that we are looking into a mirror of our past selves, and we begin to feel compassion for the people we would naturally avoid. Yet it takes only a moment before we stifle our newfound compassion by reminding ourselves how much of a struggle it was in our own lives to be rid of such negative circumstances. "Why would I want to deal with their problems? I've got enough problems of my own. I can barely deal with my own circumstances without having to deal with theirs."

So we walk away, refusing to dive into another person's misery and hopelessness because we feel that we would somehow lose something of ourselves in the process. We tell ourselves that we've worked too hard to get where we are only to give our time and energy to others in need.

Yet, truth, God's perfect truth, is not in the taking but in the giving. It's always been about the giving. "God so loved the world that he *GAVE* his one and only Son, that whoever believes in him shall not perish but have eternal life" (John 3:16, emphasis added). The very way our perfect God expressed his perfect love for us was in the giving of a perfect gift—his Son, Jesus.

The world tells us that we should not give anything to anyone because we, by definition, will lose whatever it is in the process. If we give then we no longer possess, right? Wrong! God makes it very clear, however illogical it may sound, that it is in giving our lives away that we receive everything worth having. Jesus made the ridiculous sounding statement, "Whoever finds his life will lose it, and whoever loses his life for my sake will find it" (Matthew 10:39).

How can this possibly be? What are we to make of this? And what are we supposed to do with this next verse, "What good is it for a man to gain the whole world, yet forfeit his soul?" (Mark 8:36)

God tells us to pour out, give up, surrender, and he will continue to pour into us. We were never meant to be containers holding possessions, physical or emotional. According to God, we are instead broken vessels that cannot by our design collect and hoard things indefinitely. We all will leave this world with nothing, emptied of our money and possessions. Our storehouses will be siphoned off to our friends, family and even our enemies to be treasured or squandered and we will have no say in the outcome.

We all come into this world with cracks and gaping holes on all sides of our vessels. For those who don't know God, some spend their lives trying to fill their broken vessels only to have their possessions leak out of cracks in all directions. For those who insist on trying to fight the continuous loss, they find themselves leaning to one side or the other attempting in vain to find at least one corner of the vessel's foundation that has no cracks or holes. Just when they seem to have found an angle by which they can retain some of their stuff, they realize that their lives are now completely out of balance. The possessions they can contain are insignificant, provide little if any happiness and simply drain them of too much energy trying to maintain their position. Even worse, any attempt at filling their vessel with more stuff only forces them to accept the reality that the pitiful puddle of possessions at the bottom of the vessel is all they can collect, for every effort at increasing their store by even one drop results in the loss of another drop through the cracks and holes that lie on every side.

For these people, one of two things happens. Some become distraught, despondent and depressed. They surmise that the world is mean and cruel. They conclude that they will never get a fair shake in life, that they are unwilling members of the unlucky masses in society that will never get ahead in life. Their hopes fade and their dreams die. They conclude that life is about nothing more than survival.

Others, in their pride, become obstinate and stubborn. They fight what will always be a losing battle to retain and even increase their possessions. They learn through trial and error that they can temporarily increase the volume in their container by working seventy hours a week, or by manipulating or stealing from others. They become grossly self-involved and will say things such as, "You have to look out for number one. Nothing is free in this life and everybody's out to get you. You have to take what you can get by whatever means necessary." These people fight to hold onto the idea that possessions equal happiness, and they pursue that lie to the destruction of their friendships, family and their emotional and physical well-being.

How does this lifestyle affect us as believers? Sadly, there are many of us who are distraught, despondent and depressed, living our lives on the take, never realizing what it means to pour ourselves out on behalf of those around us; never seeking out opportunities to provide for the physical, emotional, or spiritual needs of others. Confusion overtakes us. We become perplexed. Believing that salvation is like everything else in life, something to be possessed and hoarded, even hidden from others, we share God's grace with no one. Many of us, after some time, begin to wonder who would want what we possess anyway. We experience none of the joy God promises. Abundant life eludes us. Ironically, the abundance of life and joy that is promised is missing from our life because we tried to hoard it in the first place! The joy we possessed at our first encounter with God became atrophied for lack of expression. Because it was not given away, it simply faded away.

Salvation, once received, must be quickly given away. Joy once experienced must be expressed. Those who give their God-saturated lives away are the ones who become saturated again. Like a sponge that must be squeezed after it becomes soaked in order for it to be used again, so must we release all of God's love out to others so that we might be saturated, filled to overflowing yet again, and so on. We all know what happens to a bloated sponge that is left on the counter for a time. The fluid in the sponge evaporates slowly into the air leaving the sponge dry and rigid and virtually unable to accept more fluid.

Many of us, once bloated by our salvation experience with God, instead of sharing our newfound love and joy with others, choose to keep it for ourselves only to find it slowly evaporates into nothingness. We find ourselves parched and thirsty but no longer able to receive. No longer able to give or receive, we become despondent.

Is there a solution for those of us who missed the opportunity to pour out while still filled with newfound joy? Is there a way for a believer who can no longer give or receive to experience a life of joyous giving? Yes. But we first need to understand the severity of our condition. We must come to terms with the battle we face.

5
Lives Lived on the Take

Lives are lived on the take. We take from our friends emotionally and never give back. Our jobs are about giving the absolute least of ourselves while squeezing as much as we can from our employers. We see relationships for what we can get from our counterpart versus what we have to give in return. As long as what we get is greater than what we give, we stay. But the moment our friend seems to be taking more from us than we are giving, we decide the relationship costs too much and we bail. Our romantic relationships are nothing more than an effort at taking something physically from the other to satisfy our own physical and emotional needs. Sex becomes a possession to be taken from the other through manipulation, if necessary. We suck the marrow out of others in a futile effort to increase our store, only to find that while we were busy siphoning from another person's container, ten other "friends" were all the time siphoning from our supply. We are left empty.

Whether we become hopeless and depressed in the beginning and lose our drive for life, or we stubbornly fight to fill our vessels, closing our eyes to the cracks and holes, we end up in the same place in the end—broken and empty. In either case we never poured out to others, either because we saw that there was nothing there to give or we were too busy trying to take.

Yet God has always had another plan, another opportunity. He never tells us to try to take all we can get. He instead tells us to give everything we possess. He attempts to show us that we should actually pour our lives and our possessions out to others while expecting nothing in return! He then has the audacity to promise that if we will actually give up everything with no expectation of return, then we will actually find the joy and peace and contentment we have always strived to get on the take. God promises us,

> Give, and it will be given to you. A good measure, pressed down, shaken together and running over, will be poured into your [vessel]. For with the measure you use, it will be measured to you (Luke 6:38).

This irony is too great for any nonbeliever to accept, but it is also too great for most Christians to accept completely. Believers pour out to others but still do so with an unsure heart, and rarely is it poured out without expecting anything in return. Many of us lack the faith to believe this truth in the extreme. We, instead, pour out of our perceived excess. We pour out because we believe that what we have coming from our paycheck or our other relationships will at least replace what we have given.

God wants every believer to realize that, although we are broken vessels, we can actually be filled to the point that we are "running over" by his waterfall of blessing. He is the only source for that kind of abundant life, and he is the only one who can fill us. He wants us to place our broken vessels under his downpour so that we are not only filled, but his blessings are pouring out of every crack and hole in our containers as well as over the rim in all directions.

We realize to our surprise that our cracks and holes actually become tributaries on a God-created river of blessing. Those very cracks that we despised so much now direct the overflowing love of God to so many around us—our friends, coworkers, family—even our enemies. We learn that as long as we place ourselves under the endless flow of God's grace we are able to actually pour out indiscriminately on all those around us without expecting anything from them in return. We understand that we now should not even ask for something in return for we would have no place to put it! Then, if someone insists on giving back to us for what God has done through us, we graciously accept the gift only to add it to the river of blessing we have become. The gift we receive from them does not become something we hoard and guard but something to give away freely yet again.

Realizing this paramount truth, we no longer look at those around us in need and decide we cannot help. We no longer prioritize the people in our lives and decide whom we will help first, if at all. We are no longer preoccupied with ourselves, but we can now sincerely take on the attitude of Paul when he told the Philippians to:

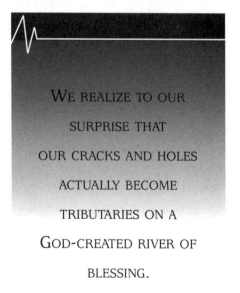

WE REALIZE TO OUR SURPRISE THAT OUR CRACKS AND HOLES ACTUALLY BECOME TRIBUTARIES ON A GOD-CREATED RIVER OF BLESSING.

> Do nothing out of selfish ambition or vain conceit, but in humility consider others better

than yourselves. Each of you should look not only to your own interests, but also to the interests of others (Philippians 2:3–4).

My son, Parker, has always loved the water. One of his favorite games as a little boy was to have Daddy douse him with the water hose in the backyard as he pretended to avoid the spray. He loved the cool water and I loved providing the entertainment. My wife, Julie, would sit and watch us and laugh with a book in one hand and a cold glass of water in the other.

The fun would continue as long as the hose remained connected to the spigot. If I were to disconnect the hose from the spigot there would be very little water left in the body of the hose to pour out and soon the hose would fall limp with only a few drops of water dropping from its mouth. I would lose out on the joy of providing the entertainment while Parker would lose out on the joy of the cool spray. So I always made sure that the hose remained connected to the spigot so I could continue to pour out to my son.

One day Parker decided he wanted to play. My wife and I were both in our lounge chairs and I didn't want to get up to turn on the spigot so I grabbed my wife's glass of water and poured it out on Parker. He laughed but wanted more. But there was no more water in the glass. Julie had no more water to quench her thirst, I had no more water to pour on my son and Parker had no more water with which to cool himself. My only option was to go to the source and turn on the spigot so I could spray him with it. Parker got all the playtime he could handle, I had a great time, and Julie had as much water as she could drink!

When we remain attached to the Source of all blessings, we are able to pour out on others with no limits. If we choose to disconnect from the Source, we begin to improvise, taking the blessings from someone else, emptying them in the process, pouring what little there is out on another, only to leave all three empty and wanting more. The *only* way to be a constant source of blessing to others is to first attach to the Source, be filled to overflowing and then you are able and willing to pour out, expecting nothing from anyone in return.

As we grow to realize the importance of connecting to the Source, we realize that we have an endless supply to give, not from our own internal reserves, but, as Paul promised, "my God will meet all your needs according to his glorious riches in Christ Jesus" (Philippians 4:19). God helps us to see that he wants to help those around us and use us as the vessel to pour out *his* love—not ours—on them. We then become willing participants in this festival of giving, realizing that we cannot exhaust the supply.

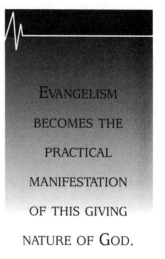

EVANGELISM BECOMES THE PRACTICAL MANIFESTATION OF THIS GIVING NATURE OF GOD.

How does this apply to the concept of evangelism? Evangelism becomes an opportunity to pour out God's love on someone who desperately needs him, rather than an obligatory act of reluctantly spending our own limited resources. We cease to see others as potential leeches that would suck us dry of our emotional and/or material resources. We move from saying, "I have to share my faith because Jesus tells me I'm obliged to do it," to saying, "I *get* to share my faith with people, diving into their misery and hopelessness so that I might reveal God's love to them. Jesus loves me so much he *lets* me build relationships with people around me who are in trouble!" Evangelism becomes the practical manifestation of this giving nature of God.

In giving we receive. In the pouring out of ourselves we are poured into. This is one of the greatest ironies of the character of God and we must attach this truth to our ongoing and ever-increasing knowledge of God. If we do not, then we will be the ones who miss out on the blessing. We will, unfortunately, be the ones sitting in the pews expecting God to perform. We will be the ones who avoid contact with troubled people. We will be the ones extremely frustrated, finding little joy in our relationship with God or others. Little progress will be made in our vain attempts at intimacy with God and the result will be anger, misery, hopelessness and disillusionment.

Do you know anyone like that?

6

Your Very Own
Spiritual Fountain of Youth

Why does God want us to be involved in his plan to put all people in right relationship with him? By now you know that the act of sharing your faith is an opportunity, maybe the greatest opportunity God gives us on this earth. It is not an obligatory box to check off in our relationship with God. It is certainly not an obligation to the church. You know now that when we share our faith we give not of ourselves but we give from an endless wellspring of love, grace, and forgiveness whose source can only be God himself.

But ...

Is this the whole story? It should be enough to know that God allows us to be involved in the greatest love story ever imagined. It should be enough that we have a God who desires to fill our cup to overflowing so that we are able to pour out to others and not expect anything in return because we are being filled completely by God. It should be enough that Jesus said, "I

"WE WRITE THIS

TO MAKE OUR

JOY COMPLETE"

(1 JOHN 1:4).

am with you always, to the very end of the age" (Matthew 28:20) so we could have confidence in his presence as we share him with others. If this was the whole story it would be enough—but there is more—a *lot more!*

There is a relatively obscure sentence in the book of 1 John. The author, John, is writing to "[his] dear children" (1 John 2:1) suggesting that he is writing to a group of fellow believers for whom he has great love and affection. The body of the letter deals mainly with determining the qualities of genuine faith. He tells his readers that genuine faith results in righteous living, love for other believers, and belief in Jesus as the Christ. In the very beginning of the letter, however, John seems to be sharing his testimony so that those who read the letter "may have fellowship with us" (1 John 1:3).

He writes:

> The one who existed from the beginning is the one we have heard and seen. We saw him with our own eyes and touched him with our own hands. He is Jesus Christ, the Word of life. This one who is life from God was shown to us, and we have seen him. And now we testify and announce to you that he is the one who is eternal life. He was with the Father, and then he was shown to us. We are telling you about what we ourselves have actually seen and heard, so that you may have fellowship with us. And our fellowship is with the Father and with his Son, Jesus Christ (1 John 1:1-3 NLT).

Whether he is telling of his personal relationship with Jesus to bless those who may read the letter and do not know Jesus, or he is simply defending his ability to impart truth to the believer, John says something quite extraordinary in verse four:

"We write this to make *our* joy complete" (1 John 1:4).

These eight words are missed by so many yet they hold the key to complete joy! John makes the claim here that the reason he is sharing the truth about Jesus is so that he and those with him might find *complete* joy!

Many places in the Bible speak of our ability to find joy in our relationship with God. In fact, the topic of joy is broached twenty times in the Old Testament and at least fourteen times in the New Testament. Yet only rarely does the writer express the idea of *complete* joy, a joy completed by some act of righteousness or imparting of truth.

The first mention of this is by Jesus himself in John 15, where he says:

> As the Father has loved me, so have I loved you. Now remain in my love. If you obey my commands, you will remain in my love, just as I have obeyed my Father's commands and remain in his love. I have told you this so that my joy may be in you and that your *joy may be complete* (John 15:9–11).

Another reference to complete joy is in the letter to the Philippians where Paul exhorts some of the first believers:

> If you have any encouragement from being united with Christ, if any comfort from his love, if any fellowship with the Spirit, if any tenderness and compassion, then *make my joy complete* by being like-minded … (Philippians 2:1–2).

The third and final reference is in the letter of 1 John. As we have already seen, John evidently shares his testimony of his personal relationship with Christ so that in simply sharing the truth he might find complete joy.

Have You Ever Experienced Complete Joy?

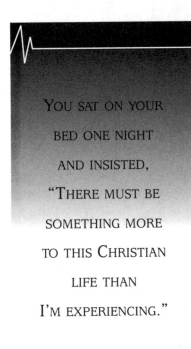

YOU SAT ON YOUR BED ONE NIGHT AND INSISTED, "THERE MUST BE SOMETHING MORE TO THIS CHRISTIAN LIFE THAN I'M EXPERIENCING."

Many of us must think back to what some call the honeymoon phase in our new-found relationship with God to remember an experience of complete joy.

What about you?

Did someone witness to you? Did you listen to a preacher on the television or radio? Maybe you just began to read the Bible one day and realized there really was a God and you didn't know him. Maybe you prayed to God that he might have mercy on you and save you from your sins and you found he was faithful to do just that. You became a child of God that day and experienced the joy of new life! Each moment from that point on seemed brighter, more real. You had found true love in your relationship with Jesus and everything was perfect. Then, one day, several months or years later, you woke up and realized that all the passion was gone or that the fire in your heart was so small you thought God should just press his fingers in around the pitiful flame and snuff it out. "No need to prolong the inevitable," you said quietly to yourself.

You sat on your bed one night and insisted, "There must be something more to this Christian life than I'm experiencing."

You whispered insistently to God expecting some response but there was no audible reply, and you became more and more resigned to the idea that this tiny, cold flame in your heart where once a bonfire burned, might just be all there is.

You still went to church every Sunday, or at least most of the time. You may even have been in a weekday Bible study. When you saw people at church and they asked how things were going, the words almost jumped out of your mouth,

"Terrible! I haven't felt close to God for years! I'm just going through the motions every day, feeling nothing inside. I've lost my passion for reading the Bible, for praying, for coming to church, and I'm sick and tired of wearing this stupid mask every time I come to church that tells everybody 'I'm fine' when I'm not!"

But you forced the words down deep inside, and you flatly replied, "Things are fine, how about you?"

If any of this is familiar at all, listen up. A huge piece of this thing we call the Christian walk is sharing our faith with other people. As Christians we will not experience all that God wants us to experience on this earth until we begin to share what we have freely received from God in the gift of salvation. God reminds us, "Freely you have received, freely give" (Matthew 10:8). The abundant, passionate, lottery-winning life that God promises in his Word is real and is attainable. But a major ingredient in the abundant life is evangelism. John shows us this truth in his tiny but tremendous statement that in sharing Jesus our joy is made complete!

Mom Never Taught Me How to Cook

A few years back I was craving chocolate chip cookies. (I crave chocolate chip cookies all the time, not just every few years but ... well, you get the point.) Not the pre-mixed kind you get in the freezer section at the grocery store; I wanted home-made cookies. I wanted the kind that you mix together in a bowl, mixing in each ingredient one by one. I imagined getting to the point where I started pouring in the chocolate chips, eating at least one chip for every ten I poured into the mix, then spooning up some of the mix and taking a delicious bite of the cookie dough before it found its way into little scoops on the baking sheet. The fact that I had never made chocolate chip cookies on my own didn't stop me. I found a box of cookie mix in the pantry and right next to it a bag of Hershey's Chocolate Chips. I was on my way to cookie heaven.

GOD REMINDS US, "FREELY YOU HAVE RECEIVED, FREELY GIVE" (MATTHEW 10:8).

I read the recipe carefully and added each ingredient listed on the box to my growing collection on the counter.

"Eggs ... eggs ... " I said as I rummaged through the refrigerator. "I can't have everything on the list but eggs!"

I looked back at all of the ingredients on the table and decided that one ingredient couldn't make that much difference. I reasoned that more butter and more water would replace the eggs quite nicely, and soon the baking sheet was full of little scoops of cookie dough headed for the pre-heated oven.

My mouth was watering for the first batch to come out of the oven. I couldn't wait to take my first bite of a hot, soft, chewy cookie. I took them out one minute early. I couldn't take it any more! As I set the baking sheet on top of the stove I knew something wasn't right. The cookies looked a little—pale. I took a spatula and slid one of the cookies off the sheet and onto my hand. I took a bite. It was *awful*! How could one ingredient make that much difference? Eggs were just one of the many ingredients, yet they proved to be a rather important part of the recipe. I learned a valuable lesson—every ingredient is important to any recipe, but some are more important than others!

I hear people all the time say, "I do everything in my relationship with God but witness," as though just one missing ingredient in their Christian walk won't make a difference; as though reading more scripture or being more involved in church activities can replace the ingredient of evangelism. Friend, every ingredient is important in our relationship with God but some are more important than others. How can I say this with such certainty? Easily. John reveals the paramount importance of witnessing in our Christian walk by defining evangelism as the only (specific) command of God that brings us complete joy!

Other than Jesus' charge for all believers to remain in his love, and Paul's charge to the Philippian believers to be like-minded, complete joy comes from sharing the truth of Jesus. An absolutely essential ingredient in our Christian walk is the ingredient of evangelism. So, if you wonder why you have little or no passion in your relationship with God, if you are just going through a set of religious exercises each day insisting that there must be something more to this thing called Christianity, don't miss this truth. Chances are very good you are not

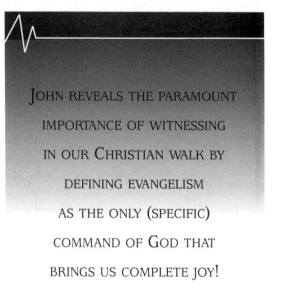

JOHN REVEALS THE PARAMOUNT IMPORTANCE OF WITNESSING IN OUR CHRISTIAN WALK BY DEFINING EVANGELISM AS THE ONLY (SPECIFIC) COMMAND OF GOD THAT BRINGS US COMPLETE JOY!

sharing your faith with other people regularly. You are not buying into the idea that when we give to others we give from God's inexhaustible supply, not our own limited resources. Do you continue to insist that evangelism is an obligation rather than the greatest of spiritual opportunities? Do you still see those who share their faith as rare, even a little strange? Do you still think that evangelism is a gift for a select few believers and that you are not one of them?

"I Don't Have the Gift of Evangelism"

For those who answered "yes" to the last question, your lack of involvement in other people's lives is simply a matter of perception. Yes, evangelism is a gift according to Paul in his letter to the Ephesians (Ephesians 4:11). Those endowed with this gift are able to publicly proclaim the Good News to the masses and watch as God reaps a plentiful harvest from the spoken word. Peter is a perfect example of one who has this evangelistic gift. In Acts chapter two, Peter addresses a massive crowd and in response to his public proclamation of the Gospel 3,000 were saved.

You may indeed not have the *gift* of evangelism. Yet, *every believer* is called to share the Good News with those around him. Jesus' charge to his disciples on the hilltop to "make disciples ... baptize ... [and] teach" (Matthew 28:19) was a charge for every believer to share his faith as an ongoing part of his life and lifestyle. We cannot excuse ourselves from this paramount ingredient in our relationship with God simply by saying that we don't have the gift of evangelism. We are all given the opportunity to involve ourselves in God's plan to reconcile the world to himself.

Complete joy then comes from freely giving as we have freely received. Complete joy manifests itself in the believer who pours God's love out on others indiscriminately. If you desire complete joy, if you have lost your passion, if life seems less than abundant—tell unbelievers about Jesus! I know this sounds too simple and almost trivial but I believe that is why most people never see this truth. The same simplicity exists in the truth of salvation: "everyone who calls on the name of the Lord will be saved" (Romans 10:13).

Too simple? No, just simple enough. You may wonder, "Can it possibly be that I've missed this idea that passion comes from sharing Jesus with others? Have I been searching for an ever more intimate relationship with God only to miss something so simple?" If you are one of the many Christians in the church today who don't share their faith, then, *yes!* You have missed out on one of the most significant pieces of the Christian pie. God wants you to know the joy that comes from simply sharing the Gospel. Read his words again: "We write this to make our joy complete."

7
Spiritual CPR

Imagine you are driving in your car alone. The clock on the dash shows 2 a.m. You are on a long, straight stretch of highway that seems to extend forever in front of you. You're bored and decide to call a friend who stays up late, but as you reach over for your cell phone you realize it's not there. Then you remember that you left it on the counter back at the house.

As you reach down to change the radio station, you realize that you haven't seen a car for over thirty minutes on either side of the highway. A few long minutes later your high beams illuminate something strange to your tired eyes. Off in the distance, underneath an overpass ... it looks like ... three, no four cars ...

Bad wreck!

As you get closer to the pile-up you catch a glimpse of something to your right and lean over the passenger seat as you drive by at a snail's pace. Stretching to see the shoulder along the right side of the road—you see him. All you can make out is a body lying face down, not moving. You stomp your foot on the brake pedal, stopping abruptly and throw the car into reverse. Backing up, you instinctively switch to low beams. As you get ready to turn and shine the headlights on the body, you reach for your cell phone, forgetting again that the phone is at home.

With no way to call 911 and no cars coming from either direction, your only choice is to get out and check the body.

"How do I do CPR? How many breaths ... how many times do I push on his chest? I've seen it on TV but I *have no idea what I'm doing*! Wait a minute, he's probably just hurt, and maybe hurt bad, but he's probably breathing."

As you talk to yourself out loud, you nervously walk to the front of the car. A few feet away from the body of what you decide must be a boy, about eighteen years old, you get a sick feeling in your stomach that things might be worse than you'd hoped.

With your shadow falling across the torso of the lifeless young man, you again look in both directions hoping to see lights, hoping for help, but there's nothing. Your breathing gets louder and shallower, your palms sweat, the motor of your car is disturbingly loud. You turn the boy over so he's lying on his back, and, almost afraid of what you will hear, or not hear, you place your ear against his chest ... nothing. You quickly put your ear to his mouth hoping to hear or feel even the slightest breath, but you feel nothing, you hear ... nothing.

You nearly hyperventilate yourself, so you take a deep breath between the shallow ones, clasp your hands together and count. "One, two, three, four, five ... " as you push on his chest.

Reluctantly, you place your mouth over his and exhale deeply into his mouth until you see his chest rise. After every three or four push-breathe-push cycles, you listen for a heartbeat, straining to hear over the pounding of your own heart. You put your ear over his mouth hoping to hear even the weakest of breaths, but your own breathing is so loud it confuses you.

"No heartbeat ... no breathing! Come on!"

With each push and with each breath you feel your own body tiring. It feels as if hours have gone by but you glance at your watch and see that it's only been twenty minutes!

Just as you're about to give up you lean down to listen to his chest one last time.

"That's ... a heartbeat and ... it's not mine!" The young man begins to take shallow breaths but he is definitely breathing! You sit back on your heels, exhausted, and all you can say to yourself is, "I just brought a dead man back to life. This guy was dead ... and now he's *alive!*"

Eventually another car slows to a stop, calls 911, and in forty-five minutes the ambulance arrives. In time, you are on your way. In shock and disbelief you arrive back at your house. What is the first thing you're going to do? *Call somebody!* You have to tell someone what happened. Nobody will ever believe it!

"Who can I call ... who's awake at 4:15 a.m.? No one, that's who. I'll call Mom!" You pick up the phone, hear a few rings and your mother answers, sounding a little confused.

"Mom, it's Todd! What are you doing?"

"I'm sleeping! It's 4:15 in the morning. What's wrong?"

"Nothing, Mom. You won't believe what just happened. Go ahead. Guess! You'll *never* guess! I just gave CPR to a dead man and brought him back to life! Can you believe it?"

It's All a Matter of Perspective

An event like that would change your perspective on life forever. It would become a stone marker in your life you would never forget. Many years after the event, as a grandparent, you would put your grandkids on your lap and tell them all about how Grandpa/Grandma brought a dead man back to life. Why? There is something very significant about the line between life and death. Only a few people get to venture so close to that line. Yet in this scenario, you touched it, even reached over it and brought someone back. Your life would never be the same.

We rarely drive or walk up on physical catastrophes like the one described above. In all likelihood we will never have the opportunity to perform CPR successfully and revive another human being. Yet something similar happens to us almost every day of our lives. We may not face physical catastrophes every day, but we do encounter spiritual catastrophes almost daily—people who are spiritually dead—not dying, but dead—all around us. They are "dead in [their] ... sins" (Ephesians 2:1) and have no hope. They possess no heavenly heartbeat, no eternal breath.

> WE MAY NOT FACE PHYSICAL CATASTROPHES EVERY DAY, BUT WE DO ENCOUNTER SPIRITUAL CATASTROPHES—PEOPLE WHO ARE SPIRITUALLY DEAD—NOT DYING, BUT DEAD—ALL AROUND US.

Yet we don't stop to offer assistance. Instead we pass by, offering nothing, even though we see no help coming in any direction for them. We tell ourselves that surely someone who knows how to *really* witness will come soon and help them. We excuse ourselves from the crisis by claiming that we don't know enough Scripture or that we wouldn't know what to say. We convince ourselves that evangelism isn't our gift and that we're not responsible for the condition of this person. Then, with no help in sight, we walk by, never even giving them a chance to hear the life-giving truth that comes from a relationship with Jesus. We miss out on the opportunity to give what I call "Spiritual CPR." Just as you might have beaten on the chest and breathed into the mouth of the dead man in the story, you have the opportunity to press the word of God into the heart of a spiritually dead friend.

Nothing is more life changing than watching a spiritually dead person come to life. Not even the act of CPR on a lifeless body can compare to giving spiritual CPR to a lifeless soul. Just as the scenario above would be a significant marker in your life, so would the act of sharing the Gospel with someone who possessed no spiritual life and then watching God place inside them their first eternal breath! Nothing will change you more than watching someone who has heard the good news pray to be forgiven, then raise his or her head, wipe the tears from his eyes and begin to breathe eternally.

Until you have experienced this, you have not experienced all that God has to offer you.

Yet, ironically, you don't have to see someone breathe his or her first eternal breath to experience complete joy. Notice in his letter John says, "We *write* this [to you] to make our joy complete."

He doesn't write, "We hope to hear back from you so our joy can be complete."

In simply sharing the truth about Jesus we find complete joy! We do not have to wait for a person to respond to our witnessing. In the simple act of witnessing God promises complete joy! Many wrongly believe that Jesus called his disciples to save people, but he is very clear that he does the saving—we are only to be witnesses. Being a witness takes the pressure off us and puts the responsibility all on God.

For example, when we are called to be witnesses in a courtroom we are

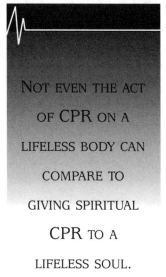

NOT EVEN THE ACT OF CPR ON A LIFELESS BODY CAN COMPARE TO GIVING SPIRITUAL CPR TO A LIFELESS SOUL.

only responsible for "telling the truth, the whole truth and nothing but the truth." We are not on the witness stand to tell a convincing story or to use colorful words. We are there to tell the facts and only the facts. Many times it takes two or three or even twenty witnesses before the facts become clear and the judge or jury can make a decision.

In the same way, God calls us to go out and make disciples by sharing the truth, the whole truth, and nothing but the truth about him to others. He then decides how many more witnesses he will put in front of those to whom we witness before they accept or deny Jesus. If we get off the witness stand and they have not reached a decision about Jesus, we have not failed. We have actually found great success, and with it, complete joy. God is responsible for our friend's salvation and we are responsible only to share the truth of Jesus. In effect, we are only responsible to press the word of God into an unbelieving person's heart by speaking truth. God has taken on the responsibility of breathing life into his or her lifeless soul when he chooses.

8

"That's My Cover"

M y wife, Julie, and I were lying on the couch watching reruns of *Charlie's Angels* (okay, so we were a little bored) and I made a comment to my wife.

"When I was nine years old, this show made total sense to me, but now it just seems ridiculous!"

Julie replied, "This is where I say, 'What do you mean, honey?'" My wife knows me too well.

"Well, when I was nine years old, it was totally reasonable that three young ladies would wait by the intercom in their office for Charlie to call with their next assignment. One week Charlie would call and say, 'Angels, your next job is to go undercover at a law firm where millions of dollars have been extorted. You will pose as attorneys while solving the extortion crime.' Off they'd go, not as janitors or secretaries, but as attorneys. And not just average attorneys, but they would be trying to win nationally covered cases with absolutely no law background at all, at the same time they were solving the extortion crime!"

Julie got a little impatient at my extensive reasoning and demanded, "What's the point?"

"I'm getting there! Think about it, honey, one week they are attorneys and the next week Charlie calls and says, 'Angels, there's been a murder at an aerobics studio. I want you three to go undercover as aerobics instructors so you can infiltrate the establishment and catch the murderer. Oh, and one more thing, the studio is hosting the National Aerobics Championships so you will be entering the contest as well.' So, they not only enter the championship—they win it! What's up with that? One week they are successful attorneys, the next week national aerobics champions? And this happens every week for an entire season?"

"Honey, it's a TV show. Quit being so critical. *Is* there a point to all of this?"

That's when I explained to my lovely wife how I had been thinking a lot about that janitor in that church who changed my life forever. That's when I explained that I was struggling with the depth of his simple reply, "That's my cover."

I said, "Charlie's Angels are sent into different places *under-cover*, to do their jobs well enough, to stay around long enough to solve the crime. In other words, their 'cover' allows them to be placed right in the middle of the action, not so they can be attorneys or aerobics instructors, but so they can be successful at their *real* assignment. That's what that old janitor at the church was trying to tell me! God had called him on the 'intercom' to tell him that his assignment was to share Jesus with people around him and that God was placing him undercover as a janitor to help him accomplish his assignment. Get it? Realizing his true purpose, he knew that he would have to do his janitorial duties well enough to stay around long enough to meet up with his next assignment—someone who didn't know Jesus!"

The janitor's words came back to me: "My job all my life has been sharing Jesus with lost folks, like you were preaching about in the sermon. This mop and this bucket ... *that's my cover.*"

"Honey," I said, "this is huge! That janitor really got it! He never got bored with his job because he knew it was nothing more than his cover. His true job was 'to save that which was lost' (Matthew 18:11 NASB). He saw the big picture. He realized his cover and knew of his loftier assignment and that gave him—JOY!"

"Leave it up to you," Julie said with a wry smile, "to discover and assimilate profound truth from a janitor and a few episodes of *Charlie's Angels!*"

My wife saw the implications and suggested I meditate on it further, possibly somewhere other than my current position lying right behind her on the couch. So I went into my office, realizing that there was much more to all of this. I understood for the first time what that janitor was trying to tell me with those three words. I suddenly saw a nation of Christians unaware of their true assignment, and because of their confusion, spending untold time and energy complaining about their dead-end jobs and their inadequate paychecks. I remembered the hundreds of people I'd spoken to over the past several years who were actually mad at God for not rescuing them from the terribly menial or downright boring jobs they worked. They would say, "If God loves me, why won't he get me out of this terrible environment I'm in at my job? My boss is a jerk and there aren't any Christians in my company."

"That's the point!" I said to myself.

God has placed us in these dark and hopeless environments precisely *because* we are God's children. We've done nothing to anger God; we are not being punished. No! We are being rewarded with an opportunity to shine the bright light of Jesus in the dark cave we call our job. If we perceive our job as menial and/or boring then our purpose is to do our menial, boring job well enough, to stay around long enough, to build deep relationships with those who are spiritually dead around us!

(Colossians 3) Sadly, many of us are so entangled in our own bitterness about our circumstances that we fail to become aware of our true assignments. Every time we pass up an opportunity to share our faith, we miss out on knowing the complete joy God desires for us. At the same time, those who need to hear the truth remain in the darkness because we are blinded by our earthly circumstances, by our pride and by our skewed sense of entitlement. A great example of this kind of spiritual blindness is in 2 Kings where the enemy surrounds the great prophet Elisha and his servant:

> YOUR JOB, FOR EXAMPLE, IS SIMPLY ONE OF MANY CIRCUMSTANCES IN YOUR LIFE THAT GOD USES TO BRING YOU FACE TO FACE WITH YOUR NEXT "ASSIGNMENT"

When the servant of the man of God got up and went out early the next morning, an army with horses and chariots had surrounded the city. "Oh, my lord, what shall we do?" the servant asked. "Don't be afraid," the prophet answered. "Those who are with us are more than those who are with them." And Elisha prayed, "O Lord, open his eyes so he may see." Then the Lord opened the servant's eyes, and he looked and saw the hills full of horses and chariots on fire all around Elisha (2 Kings 6:15–17).

The servant was overwhelmed by his earthly circumstances even to the point of being unable to see the mighty work of God around him. He saw his circumstances as hopeless and cried out to Elisha. Elisha prayed that God would open his servant's eyes. His physical eyes were already opened but his spiritual eyes were tightly shut. Then God opened his spiritual eyes so that he could witness the truth of his circumstances, which in his case was God's army saturating the hills around the city in all directions.

My prayer for you is that God will open your spiritual eyes and ears to see and hear what is there for you to experience in your present circumstances. Your immediate circumstances, such as your job or the neighborhood in which you live, are not what God wants you to focus on any more than I would find it necessary that you focus on the color of my Bible cover as I'm preaching to you. Your job, for example, is simply one of many circumstances in your life that God uses to bring you face to face with your next "assignment"—a person in your life who has yet to be introduced to Jesus!

As Christians, we must begin to see our life circumstances—from our jobs to the people we see regularly at the grocery store to the people who just moved in next-door—as providential and therefore extremely important circumstances rather than random and unfortunate realities of our not-so-special lives. We are in this world but not of this world and thus we are freed from defining our lives by our job titles, money in the bank, or sphere of influence. Ours is a higher calling, a paramount mission that cannot be defined in terms of hours on the clock, titles, or possessions. Ours is a mission that can only be carried out by those who are truly children of God and who have been freed from the blinding fiction of life's circumstances. We are children of God who have been stationed on this earth as visitors bearing an incredible, indescribable gift (2 Corinthians 9:15) for

THIS IS THE STUFF OF LEGEND. THIS IS THE STUFF OF GOD.

anyone who would hear and respond. This is the stuff of legend. This is the stuff of God.

Bottom line—Jesus commanded us to "make disciples … baptize … and teach" (Matthew 28:19) because he loves us with a perfect love and wants to share with us the joy that he himself experiences as his kingdom is expanded one soul at a time. He wants us to be freed from the chains of our own perceived limitations, whatever they may be, and to go and make disciples by sharing *his* truth using *his* power. This is the great secret of the universe—to know God and to make him known! Most of us in the church have either never been told of this great secret or we have chosen not to listen (or not to believe).

A Sandwich Full of Truth

When Julie and I were first married we moved into a small apartment that could more appropriately be described as a two-story envelope. Downstairs was the living room and the kitchen and upstairs was the bedroom and the bathroom. People would ask me how big our apartment was and in my usual understated way I'd say, "Twelve square feet—but that's just the downstairs area. There's a whole area upstairs I haven't measured yet."

A couple of weeks after we got back from our honeymoon I was lying on the couch in the living room watching TV. The couch was on one wall of the living room and the television was on the opposite wall, but I didn't need a remote control to change the channel. The room was so narrow I could reach the TV on the opposite wall without leaving my prone position on the couch!

Julie came downstairs, slid between me and the TV and asked if I would like for her to make me a sandwich. I said, "Yeah, that'd be great! How about a turkey sandwich?"

She'd never made me a sandwich before and, in my mind, sandwich making is more of an art than a simple repetitive process. I was, however, able to release what had been an area in my life reserved only for me, for the simple reason that I thought Julie (and all women for that matter) knew about the Universal Law of Sandwich Making. This law states very simply that, "Names are ascribed to sandwiches based on the quantity of the ingredients." For example, a peanut butter and jelly sandwich has equal amounts of peanut butter and jelly, therefore, each ingredient gets equal billing in the name. I was totally bewildered when I found out that most women were not aware of this law.

As she turned the corner into the kitchen my mind conjured up a beautiful picture of the ultimate turkey sandwich—two or three half-inch thick slices of turkey and a nice thick slice of whatever cheese happened to be in the fridge, all wrapped inside two hearty slices of wheat bread.

"Meat, cheese, bread!" I said to myself as I beat my chest.

According to the U.L.S.M. (Universal Law of Sandwich Making) what my imagination had created was truly a turkey sandwich.

My mouth-watering food fantasy was interrupted, though, when I began to hear strange and unfamiliar noises coming from the kitchen—utensils clanging, drawers opening and closing and what sounded like the tops of jars being unscrewed and dropped onto the counter.

"Maybe she's making something for herself," I murmured as the orchestra of otherworldly sounds from the kitchen faded and I heard, "Honey, do you want to eat out in the living room?"

"Sounds good."

Around the corner she came with two identical sandwiches, one in each hand. First I spied the entire head of lettuce that seemed to dominate the concoctions on each plate. Then I became frighteningly aware of what looked like one or even two whole tomatoes! Dripping off the lettuce was something I had seen before but never in my life imagined being included on a sandwich destined for my mouth—salad dressing!

"Where's the turkey?"

"It's in there, honey."

Have you ever seen those packages of deli meat hanging in the refrigerated section at the grocery store? You know, the ones that have forty see-through slices of meat in each one of those tiny little packages? My wife is convinced to this day that each package will make forty individual sandwiches! So, somewhere in this monstrosity on my plate was one single little see-though slice of turkey that represented all of the meat in my sandwich. If I were to take a cross section of the sandwich in front of me, peering in on its ingredients, I would be forced to conclude, based on the Universal Law of Sandwich Making, that this was not a turkey sandwich but a salad sandwich! Although my wife was calling it a turkey sandwich, turkey was what I found least in the sandwich!

Just because you call a dog a cat, doesn't change the fact that a dog is a dog, not a cat. In the same way, most of us reading this book call ourselves Christians. For some of us, though, if we're honest with ourselves, the Christian label we give ourselves is what we find least in our lives. If we took a cross section of our lives, we would find few of the ingredients that make up a passionate and fulfilling Christian life. We call ourselves Christians, but what we really have is a "salad sandwich." I'm not implying that we may not really be born again children of God who have an address in heaven waiting for us. What I am saying is that many of us are leaving out a main ingredient of our Christian experience, the topic we have been discussing throughout this book—evangelism!

We must cross the great chasm of uncertainty, doubt and fear by having faith that God will not only create the opportunities for us to share our faith, but that he will also give us the words to say, the actions to take and the expressions of love to make to our unbelieving relatives, friends or enemies so that they can start their own intimate and eternal relationships with God, and we can, at the same time, experience true and complete joy.

Why do we share our faith? To experience the complete joy

that God promises us in our relationship with him. These are truths that should be obvious to all of us but have eluded many in the present-day church.

9
For Joy to Be Complete, It Must Be Shared

D o you remember what it felt like to get an *A+* on an assignment in school? As soon as you saw the grade you had to nudge your friend sitting in front of you so he could turn around and see your grade. Whether it was a winning touchdown, a good grade on a paper or an especially good hair day, we all desire to tell someone about it. There's a sense inside us that the victory is not complete, the grade is not real, until it is shared.

My wife's lifelong dream was to honeymoon at Disney World. Of all the places you could go for a honeymoon she chose a theme park. I wasn't one to destroy the dream of my soon-to-be wife, so I made all the arrangements and the day after our wedding we were off to the land of Mickey Mouse, Donald Duck, and kids—lots and lots of kids. My expectations were low, to say it mildly, but by the time our week at the Magic Kingdom was over I wanted desperately to stay just a few more days.

We boarded the plane, however, and headed home to start our life together. I looked at Julie and said, "I can't wait to get back and tell all the guys at work how much fun we had at Disney World!"

My first day back to work after my honeymoon I spent every spare moment (and some not-so-spare) telling my coworkers how much fun Julie and I had at Disney World and how I'd like to go back. My experience was simply too wonderful to keep inside. I was unable to hold it in. People around me were going to hear about my honeymoon whether they wanted to or not. The joy inside me had to come out.

In contrast, many Christians who have experienced an event far greater and more profound than a winning touchdown or a trip to Disney World somehow find a way to keep their personal relationship with God a secret. They decline every opportunity to share the incredible truth that they actually have a personal, one-on-one relationship with the God of the Universe. As a result, they live a quiet passionless life of missed opportunities. These same people, however, will think that being in the same room with a movie star or sports figure is a life-changing experience, and they will *create* opportunities to tell their story of their brush with greatness. Ironically, in God's reality, the experience of joy comes in the *act* of sharing our salvation. In other words, the joy of salvation cannot be fully realized in our lives

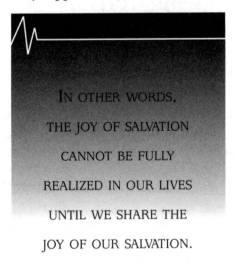

IN OTHER WORDS, THE JOY OF SALVATION CANNOT BE FULLY REALIZED IN OUR LIVES UNTIL WE SHARE THE JOY OF OUR SALVATION.

until we share the joy of our salvation. The sharing is a necessary part of the joy we experience from our salvation. Rather
than the act of sharing simply being the result of a completed
event or experience in a worldly sense, it is an essential part
of the salvation experience.

St. John and his cohorts experienced salvation through
Jesus, yet he claims in 1 John 1:4 that the joy of that salvation will
not be complete until it is expressed. I believe this strange truth
fits perfectly with God's character. The entire Bible teaches us
that our relationship with God works on an "obey, *then* gain wisdom" paradigm. God desires that we walk by *faith* not by sight
and he therefore calls us to act first in faith and then we will be
rewarded with *sight*. Yet we would rather have God give us wisdom so it will make sense for us to obey. We want to see around
the corner to know what's coming before we take the next step.

"God, if I witness to my father will he get angry?"

"Is this the right time to talk to my best friend about Jesus?"

"God, are you going to reveal yourself to my friend today if
I witness to him?"

No. God has a different plan. He commands us to walk, run,
even leap ahead in faith without knowing many times what the
result will be, all of this so that we will rely on him rather than
an empty religion or self-help philosophy. My favorite example
of this is in the book of Joshua:

> And the LORD said to Joshua, "Today I will begin to
> exalt you in the eyes of all Israel, so they may know that
> I am with you as I was with Moses. Tell the priests who
> carry the ark of the covenant: 'When you reach the edge
> of the Jordan's waters, go and stand in the river.'"
>
> Joshua said to the Israelites, "Come here and listen
> to the words of the LORD your God. This is how you will
> know that the living God is among you ... as soon as the
> priests who carry the ark of the LORD—the Lord of all
> the earth—set foot in the Jordan, its waters flowing

downstream will be cut off and stand up in a heap." So when the people broke camp to cross the Jordan, the priests carrying the ark of the covenant went ahead of them. *Now the Jordan is at flood stage all during harvest. Yet as soon as the priests who carried the ark reached the Jordan and their feet touched the water's edge, the water from upstream stopped flowing.* It piled up in a heap a great distance away, at a town called Adam in the vicinity of Zarethan, while the water flowing down to the Sea of the Arabah was completely cut off. So the people crossed over opposite Jericho. *The priests who carried the ark of the covenant of the LORD stood firm on dry ground in the middle of the Jordan,* while all Israel passed by until the whole nation had completed the crossing on dry ground (Joshua 3:7–10, 13–17).

Did you notice it? Did you see the example of the "faith then sight" principle?

Imagine you were one of the priests instructed by Joshua to carry the ark of the covenant up to the edge of the Jordan River as it rushed by at flood stage. What if you were one of the two priests given charge to take hold of the acacia wood poles at the front of the ark? What if the first feet to enter the floodwaters of the Jordan were going to be yours?

If I was one of those priests I might find myself looking over to my counterpart and whispering, "Pssst. Now let me get the order of events straight. We walk up to the floodwaters, ark in hand, God parts the waters *and then* we cross. Right?"

"No," would come the reply. "You and I are supposed to *walk into the rushing waters and then God is going to stop the floodwaters* on both sides and let all of the Israelites pass."

Have you ever been in a moment like that? God calls for action on your part before he performs his promise? I don't know for sure but my guess is that the two priests didn't consider their position at that point to be in any way akin to winning the priestly lottery. In fact, I would argue that they might have tried to collect on a few favors, trying desperately to get someone to stand in their place. No such luck. Yet, it was the two priests who were called to the front of the line that day who experienced two very profound things that no one else in the nation of Israel experienced: faith tested and faith *tasted*.

The priests' faith in God was tested perhaps like no other time in their lives. The priests were not called to stick their toes in the water but to step purposefully with the weight of their own bodies and the weight of the stone tablets inside the gold-encrusted ark to force all of themselves into the floodwaters. Add to all of this the weight of the expectations of 3 million Israelites.

So—they step.

Faith tested.

Even as their weight pressed their feet through the surface of the raging waters at the bank of the Jordan, just as their expectations of being pulled into the torrent reached the heights of certainty—the waters below their feet gave way to solid ground. The torrent of rushing water was simply not there any longer. They didn't blink but their eyes still could not capture the miracle. The waters were there in all their force and then they simply were no more.

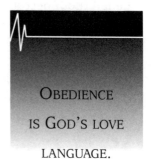

OBEDIENCE IS GOD'S LOVE LANGUAGE.

They stood firm on dry ground in the middle of the Jordan.

Faith tasted!

No doubt the priests second or third in line holding the ark were tested, asking themselves questions like, "Are they actually going to just step off into the Jordan?"

"What would I do if I were them?"

Their faith was tested indirectly and their faith increased by witnessing what God did to the floodwaters. Yet, on any

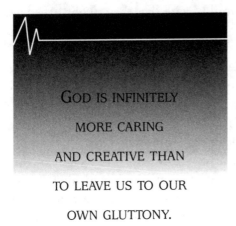

GOD IS INFINITELY

MORE CARING

AND CREATIVE THAN

TO LEAVE US TO OUR

OWN GLUTTONY.

given Sunday preachers all over the world are preaching from this passage in our times in an effort to increase the faith of the believer. And, the reading of this passage does increase the measure of faith in a believer's heart. The lottery winners, however, were the two priests in the front of a 3 million-person line, stepping not into the floodwaters of the Jordan but through the floodgates of wisdom. They tasted, touched, saw, heard, and smelled the indescribable aroma of the faith that comes from true obedience and the complete joy that comes from following God's instruction. God reminded Joshua:

> Do not let this Book of the Law depart from your mouth; meditate on it day and night, so that you may be careful to do everything written in it. Then you will be prosperous and successful (Joshua 1:8).

Jesus said,

> Whoever has my commands and obeys them, he is the one who loves me (John 14:21).

Obedience is God's love language. Our passion, purpose, joy, and faith come from doing the things of God.

Sharing our faith then, as with the priests at the edge of the Jordan, is an area, maybe *the* area for many, where our faith is tested the most. For some of us, obeying God's command to share the Good News with others is tantamount to casting our foot into the Jordan. Yet, just as God promised the Israelites, as you obey he will part the waters of insecurity and fear, and you will stand firm in your witness for Christ.

God's command: share your faith.

God's promise: complete joy.

So, as strange as this may sound, we must share our story of salvation with others before we can gain a passion for sharing our story of salvation with others. It is in the act of sharing by faith that God then instills in you a passion to share your faith!

If the entirety of our salvation experience and the joy that came from it was only in the event, we would tend to sit and bask in the truth of our relationship with the divine, becoming so bloated in the experience of our joy that we would be unable to move, like a man who gorges himself at a buffet. The problem with gorging at the buffet is that there comes a point where we no longer feel full but over-stuffed. We become uncomfortable, even sick to our stomachs. No, God is infinitely more caring and creative than to leave us to our own gluttony. He has created a divinely wonderful plan by which the joy of our salvation cannot, on its own, sustain our passion for life. We must move away from the dining table with God and go out and bring others to the feast. We can only find sustained joy, completed joy, in the act of reliving our salvation experience with others so that they, too, can begin their journey with God.

10

People Matter

A young seminary student and his best friend from high school were several years out of college, both in their early twenties. Mary, an elementary school teacher in a suburb of Dallas worked primarily with special needs children. Scott was in his third year at a seminary in the Dallas area. Mary and Scott saw each other often. They spent hours on the phone, just as they had ever since high school, and made it a habit to meet for lunch once a week.

Mary had been working at her school for over two years and although she had audited a few of Scott's classes at seminary, he had declined repeated invitations from her to visit her elementary school class.

"I get very uncomfortable with special needs children," Scott confessed with embarrassment. "And besides, you say you only have three kids in your class. What is there to see?"

Mary insisted, "We've known each other for a really long

time and all I'm asking you to do is spend one hour with me in my class with my kids. I don't think that's too much to ask."

Scott knew he would eventually have to accept Mary's invitation or risk damaging the friendship they had shared for so many years. He could sense there was no way out. He inquired, "When and where?"

A few days later, Scott was in one of his morning classes taking notes when he realized that he had nearly forgotten he was going to Mary's school in less than two hours.

"Talk about cutting it close," he whispered to himself as the professor continued lecturing.

The class let out a few minutes late but Scott still (unfortunately, he thought) had more than enough time to make it to Mary's class.

Her directions to the school were clear, as was the map of the school she'd drawn on a napkin. Mary left nothing to chance. Scott checked his watch as he approached the door to the classroom.

"Twenty minutes *early* ... great."

He walked into a rectangular classroom with a sealed cement floor and windows covering the wall opposite the door. He could see kids playing on equipment inside a gated playground.

In the room stood the teacher's desk and chair and a ten-foot portable table with three small chairs tucked under the table facing the front of the room. Not wanting to disturb anything, he found a small chair in the hall and situated himself in a back corner of the room.

A few minutes passed before he heard shuffling feet and what he imagined were backpacks dragging on the ground behind the students. His ears didn't deceive him, but his eyes weren't prepared for what he saw come through the door. An elderly lady in a multi-colored sweater and long blue skirt with reading glasses on a string around her neck entered the room first. Behind her came three young children, one behind the other with their right hands holding onto the right shoulder of the person in front of them. Two little girls walked ahead of a disheveled boy in the rear of the line. Scott saw that the girls seemed normal enough with their hair in ponytails and their backpacks placed squarely on their backs. But the little boy was somehow different. The backpack dragging across the floor was his. The girl ahead of him held his right hand to her shoulder as though he would let go if she were not mindful to keep him attached.

As they were each led to a chair at the table, Scott became even more uncomfortable.

"Will you be in here for the entire hour of class?" the lady asked Scott.

"Uh, I'm just, well, I'm a friend of Mary's and so I'm just coming by to see her."

"Would you mind sitting where you are and watching over the children until Mary arrives?"

Scott's mind scrambled for a good reason to say no, but he knew there was none.

"Sure, but do I have to do anything or ... anything?" The elderly lady assured him that all he would be responsible for is making sure they didn't leave the room.

As Scott was becoming anxious at the possibility of one of the children falling unconscious and other problematic scenarios, Mary walked into the room, caught Scott's eye and walked briskly to the back corner of the room where he sat.

"I am so very excited that you came. I wasn't sure you'd make it, but you did!"

Scott gave her a big hug.

"Some lady put me in charge of the class until you arrived. I'm glad you—arrived."

Mary quickly placed projects in front of the two girls then rolled her chair directly in front of the small boy. She began the lesson for the day.

"Hi, Tommy. How has your day been so far?"

No response from Tommy.

"Great!" said Mary. "We're going to see if this day can't get even better!"

Still no response from Tommy.

"Tommy, we're going to continue our lesson from yesterday on how to use a spoon."

Mary pulled a spoon out of her pocket, placed it in Tommy's right hand and closed his fingers around the handle.

"Now, Tommy, just like we worked on yesterday, I am going to count to three and slowly let go of your hand. All you will do is keep your fingers closed tightly around the handle of the spoon."

Mary counted to three and slowly removed her hand from around Tommy's. The spoon immediately fell to the table. Scott was on the edge of his seat as if he were watching the seventh game of the World Series in the bottom of the ninth, three balls, two strikes and a homerun needed to clinch the series. Then, "strike three!" The miracle didn't happen. The home team didn't win the game.

Strangely enough, Scott thought, Mary continued to talk to Tommy—who was obviously severely autistic and non-responsive—as though he heard every word she was saying. With sincere encouragement and hope in her voice she continued to help Tommy wrap his hand around the handle of that spoon and watch it fall to the table for what seemed to Scott a thousand times—until the bell rang signaling the end of class.

"Tommy, this was your best day yet! I can't wait until tomorrow. You'll do even better!"

Mary rose up from her chair and rolled it back behind her desk just as the same lady who guided the students into the room now took them out.

Scott stood up and walked the length of the small room and caught Mary before she could push her chair entirely under the desk.

"Mary ... "

Scott was interrupted by Mary's excited words.

"I'm thrilled that you were able to stay for the entire class!"

Scott's brow crinkled.

"Mary, what are you doing in this place? What in the world are you doing here when you have a degree in elementary education? You were top of your class. You had offers from several schools. Why this one? You could be teaching students who have a chance to make a difference in this world. I know this sounds terrible, but this is a waste of your time teaching a little autistic boy how to hold a spoon. Why are you here?"

Mary was disheartened by Scott's response and saw that he was truly blind to the work she was engaged in.

"Why do I do this? Because he matters! That little boy matters."

Mary spent the next several minutes, within the limits of what the English language would allow, attempting to explain why she was there, what she was doing and why that little boy was the *most important person in the whole world,* worthy of her undivided attention, love, respect, and time. Then she looked into Scott's eyes and made her most confusing statement.

"I am also here for me. I cannot give any amount equal to what I receive from this experience and from these relationships."

Scott learned a powerful lesson that day. The simple truth is—*people matter.* They matter to God and they should matter to us. Not for what they can do or for how they look or for what they can offer, but simply because they exist. They matter because God chose in his infinite wisdom and power to create them. They matter because God wills that they matter.

An Elite Gathering

Philip Yancey, one of my favorite authors, had the privilege of meeting and having an extended discussion with another author who has profoundly shifted, altered, affirmed, and corrected my spiritual reasoning over time, Henri Nouwen. Many people in the Christian community today are familiar with Philip Yancey. He is a contemporary writer who has etched his name into the obelisks of our time by allowing God to use him to write books such as *The Jesus I Never Knew* and *What's So Amazing About Grace?* I am not exaggerating when I say that these and other books penned by Yancey are in the personal libraries of every minister I know. Yancey is a seer of the times in which we live and prophet of the inevitable results of our corporate condition in the church world. I believe Yancey would agree with me when I say that he met a man, Nouwen, who had the same or even greater effect on him, as Yancey already has and continues to have on our generation.

Yancey sat one day among other giants in the field of Christian writing such as Richard Foster, most noted for authoring *Celebration of Discipline*, and Eugene Peterson, an author who accepted the seemingly insurmountable task of translating the Bible into the language of our day. The result of Peterson's work is *The Message*, which is a Bible translation that has done as much to get the Bible into the hands of the masses, as did Luther's translation of the Bible from Latin to German, the common language of his region, in the early 1500s.

Their conversation ebbed and flowed, eventually leading to discussion of a letter they each received from a young man seeking spiritual guidance. This same young man wrote to both Foster and Peterson requesting insights and direction. They both felt they did the best they could by written correspondence, suggesting certain books related to the subject in question. As the conversation was moving in another direction, Foster spoke up.

"This same young man contacted Henri Nouwen. You won't believe what Nouwen did," he said. "He invited this stranger to *live* with him for a month so he could mentor him in person." (Yancey, "The Holy Inefficiency of Henri Nouwen," *Christianity Today*, December 9, 1996)

At this point I want to move from the subject of evangelism in order to dig deeply into a frequently avoided truth—*people matter*. This truth is at the core of our understanding of the "why" of evangelism. It is central to our understanding of the very reason we have the opportunity to be in an eternally intimate relationship with the God of creation. To do this, let me share a summary of Nouwen's life and then parallel it to the life of Mary, the young teacher in Dallas, so that we might be able to act upon the enlightenment we receive from the experiences of these people.

Nouwen lived most of his life with prestige, power, and influence, primarily because of his writing and the fact that he taught at Notre Dame, Yale and Harvard. He rose to the highest levels in Christendom. Yet at his peak he became keenly aware that his hectic schedule was suffocating his intimacy with God. Because of this, he left the states to seek out missionary work in South America. Soon after his return, his horrid schedule resumed at a relentless pace, unaffected by his absence. Nouwen then chose to take a position at the L'Arche community in France, a home for the seriously disabled, and later became the resident priest at a similar home in Toronto, Canada, called Daybreak. He had escaped what many of us would call the church industry and immersed himself in a life of what Yancey termed "holy inefficiency."

The day of Yancey's visit also marked the twenty-sixth birthday of a young man named Adam, to whom Nouwen was given charge. The young man was unable to talk, walk, dress himself, or take charge of his own hygiene. Nouwen went on to describe in some detail the task of bathing, dressing, and feeding Adam each morning. This process consumed two hours of every twenty-four hour day.

Yancey admitted his doubts as to the wisdom of a man like Henri Nouwen spending his time performing the most menial of tasks for a young man who might not even be able to understand the sacrifice that was being made on his behalf. Yancey made an effort to broach the subject of Nouwen's chosen vocation, but Nouwen interrupted him. "I am not giving up anything," he insisted. "It is I, not Adam, who gets the main benefit from our friendship."

Nouwen later wrote about it in his book *In the Name of Jesus*:

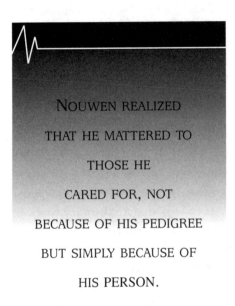

NOUWEN REALIZED THAT HE MATTERED TO THOSE HE CARED FOR, NOT BECAUSE OF HIS PEDIGREE BUT SIMPLY BECAUSE OF HIS PERSON.

The first thing that struck me when I came to live in a house with mentally handicapped people was that their liking or disliking me had absolutely nothing to do with any of the useful things I had done until then. Since nobody could read my books, they could not impress anyone, and since most of them never went to school, my twenty years at Notre Dame, Yale and Harvard did not provide a significant introduction. My considerable ecumenical experience proved even less valuable. ... Not being able to use any of the skills that had proved to be so practical in the past was a real source of anxiety. I was suddenly faced with my naked self, open for affirmations and rejections, hugs and punches, smiles and tears, all dependent simply on how I was perceived at the moment. ... These broken, wounded and completely unpretentious people forced me to let go of my relevant self—the self that can do things, show things, prove things, build things—and forced me to reclaim that unadorned self in which I am completely vulnerable, open to receive and give love regardless of any accomplishments. (p. 15–16)

In what I consider to be one of the paramount ironies of the human condition, Nouwen actually learned to receive and later give exactly what Mary, the young teacher from Dallas gave every day to her students—unconditional love. Nouwen realized that he mattered to those he cared for, not because of his pedigree but simply because of his *person*. This kind of love is forever detached from power, influence, success, or failure. It is tied neither to credibility or credential, education or fame.

So, what do these stories have to do with the "why" of evangelism? How do the experiences of Mary, the teacher in Dallas, and Henri Nouwen, the author, help us to understand why we are to seek opportunities to share our faith, share in the trials of others and experience the pain and hopelessness of those around us? It is certainly not so we can add another notch to our "evangelism belt" or so we can claim selfless service on God's behalf. No—it is for the simple fact that people have inherent value to God. People matter. They are worthy of our attention, our time and our resources because of the value that God places on them. By God's own hands, every individual has been "knit ... together in [their] mother's womb" (Psalm 139:13) and every person is "fearfully and wonderfully made" (Psalm 139:14). Ours is not to determine the value of others but to respond to them and serve them because of their eternal and immeasurable worth to God.

To put it another way, we are to treat even the "least of these" (Matthew 25:40) as we would the Christ himself. They are to be the recipients of the undying loyalty and service that we as Christians claim to offer daily to God himself. Our service to people is the greatest expression of God's light, for we "are the light of the world" (Matthew 5:14) and it is in that expression that our joy is made complete.

11

Why Does God Love Me?

People often ask me why God loves them. I confess that in the first years of my relationship with God I could not answer the question. But as I grew more mature and began to grasp the meaning and implications of God's grace through the writings of men such as Yancey and Nouwen, I found the answer to the question. I still remember waiting for months for someone to ask me that question again. Finally a young lady came up after a worship event at a youth camp.

"I still can't get a grip. Why does God love me if I've done so much bad stuff?"

With joy in my heart I smiled and leaned down so we would be eye to eye.

"Young lady, God loves you for no good reason. In fact, he loves you in spite of you and in spite of your sin and in spite of the sin you're going to do tomorrow and the next day and the next and the next."

Her facial expressions went from expressing confusion to curiosity to doubt to enlightenment to joy all in a matter of seconds. She simply walked away.

People matter to God for no good earthly reason. You are a treasured creation of God's own hands, treasured even above the angels (1 Corinthians 6:3). You matter not for what you do or for what you can contribute, but simply because God created you to be a recipient of his perfect and eternal love. He created you to be an heir to his entire kingdom, not for anything you have or have not done, will or will not do. No, he loves you with an unconditional love that you will find nowhere else but from God, in and through the person of Jesus.

The American Heritage Dictionary (4th ed., 2000) defines "unconditional" as "without conditions or limitations."

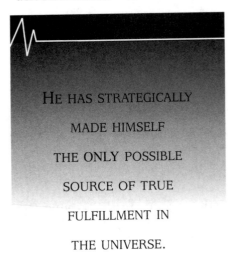

HE HAS STRATEGICALLY MADE HIMSELF THE ONLY POSSIBLE SOURCE OF TRUE FULFILLMENT IN THE UNIVERSE.

Therefore, there is no condition by which God would love you any less and there is no limit to God's love for you. His love is eternally unconditional. There is great power in the reality that not only does God love each of us with unconditional love but that he is the only source in the universe for unconditional love. He has strategically made himself the *only* possible source of true fulfillment in the universe. We are created by him and for him to be in relationship with him. In creating us he masterfully designed us with a gap, a hole in our being that only he can fill. We are born in sin and at the same time born with an insatiable appetite for that something or someone that will give us peace. In our sin we pursue the things of this world in an effort to fill our spiritual bellies, but the hunger pangs continue unaffected by our earthly indulgences. Many of us realize with utter frustration that in filling our bellies we only increase the hunger. There is no filling of the

THEY IGNORE THEIR HUNGER AND LIVE LIVES OF QUIET RESIGNATION TO THE IDEA THAT BEING FOREVER HUNGRY IS THE WAY OF MAN.

soul—until we meet the one who made himself to be the only source of satisfaction, peace and fulfillment.

I believe many in the church are totally unaware of this indescribable gift of unconditional love. This lack of knowledge is the reason I'm zeroing in on this subject of unconditional love. We must understand not just intellectually but experientially the treasure we possess in this godly love. Its value is exceedingly and abundantly greater than all of the world and everything in it. We possess it in order to offer it to those around us.

The Haves and the Have Nots

Many times we look at those in our social circles who possess more earthly treasures than we do and convince ourselves that there is no reason for them to listen to us about God. After all, they have everything the world could offer. Our false assumptions lead us to turn away, never offering our rich friend *true* wealth.

The irony of this all-too-familiar scenario would be humorous except for its dire consequence. For those of us who have never tasted worldly success, we don't realize that many times it is those who possess in abundance the things of this world whose bellies growl the loudest. For they have feasted at the buffet of worldly possession, going back for more and more, gorging on the endless feast only to become more and more famished.

Yet, in their emptiness, they have mastered the art of *looking* full. They have mastered the science of convincing themselves and everyone else they know that they are satisfied. They ignore their hunger and live lives of quiet resignation to the idea that being forever hungry is the way of man. They believe that all men are as hungry as they are and if that is the case then, they conclude, why not be the one with the most toys.

They are often ripe to hear of the hope that comes from a relationship with God. They are living lives of resignation and famine. They have drunk from every well and feasted at every table—but one. You have what they desperately desire. You have water they can drink and "never thirst" again (John 4:14). You have a personal invitation for them to sit at the "feast in the kingdom of God" (Luke 13:29). You have an eternal inheritance to offer them that they and a thousand generations before them could not amass in worldly possessions. You possess the key to genuine riches beyond their meager, earthly, material-driven imaginations.

All people matter to God. Your friends matter to God. Your family members matter to God. Your coworkers matter to God. Even your enemies matter to God. The rich and the poor—all are to be invited to the feast. All are invited to drink eternal water and we, the believers, are the bearers of the invitation to the party. We must not let assumptions get in the way. We must not let fear rob them of their inheritance and rob us of our complete joy.

Even Men Like Hitler Matter to God

I'm often asked questions like this one:

"Okay, God loves me for no good reason. But how can a guy like Hitler get to heaven after all the terrible things he did?"

I find that most people can eventually understand a God who can love *them* even though they have done, for some, unspeakable things. Yet in their still sinful nature they have a very hard time imagining a man like Hitler receiving the same grace.

There is a very important story in the Bible that deals with this perception of justice:

> For the kingdom of heaven is like a landowner who went out early in the morning to hire men to work in his vineyard. He agreed to pay them a denarius for the day and sent them into his vineyard. About the third hour he went out and saw others standing in the marketplace doing nothing. He told them, "You also go and work in my vineyard, and I will pay you whatever is right." So they went. He went out again about the sixth hour and the ninth hour and did the same thing. About the eleventh hour he went out and found still others standing around. He asked them, "Why have you been standing here all day long doing nothing?"
>
> "Because no one has hired us," they answered. He said to them, "You also go and work in my vineyard." When evening came, the owner of the vineyard said to his foreman, "Call the workers and pay them their wages, beginning with the last ones hired and going on to the first." The workers who were hired about the eleventh hour came and each received a denarius. So when those came who were hired first, they expected to receive more. But each one of them also received a denarius. When they received it, they began to grumble against the landowner. "These men who were hired last worked only one hour," they said, "*and you have made them equal to us who have borne the burden of the work and the heat*

of the day." But he answered one of them, "Friend, I am not being unfair to you. Didn't you agree to work for a denarius? Take your pay and go. I want to give the man who was hired last the same as I gave you. Don't I have the right to do what I want with my own money? Or are you envious because I am generous?" So the last will be first, and the first will be last (Matthew 20:1–16).

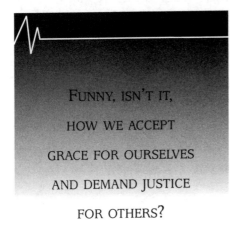

FUNNY, ISN'T IT, HOW WE ACCEPT GRACE FOR OURSELVES AND DEMAND JUSTICE FOR OTHERS?

What's your first reaction to that story? I, for one, was on the side of the workers who worked the entire day and received the same wages as the man who arrived thirty minutes before the five o'clock whistle blew. Think about it. Aren't you upset when you don't think you're getting a fair shake? Haven't you ever been in an hourly wage job where there is that one guy who seems to do nothing, gets paid the same wage you do, while you're doing everything you're supposed to do and more? "It just isn't fair," you tell yourself.

On the other hand, if we were the ones who began work at the late hour and received a full day's pay, we might feel a bit sorry for those who worked all day for the same pay. But we would get over those fleeting feelings of guilt and gladly accept the unearned pay from the landowner.

Hitler is a different breed, however. He took the job in the morning, killed the landowner, forced the other workers into slavery and killed those who defied him. Then he proceeded to burn the vines that produced the fruit and sent word to every landowner on the borders of his vineyard that they, too, would pay, serve, submit, or be destroyed. What do we do with our God who forgave us and seems to be unwilling to deem even a man like Hitler to be too sinful for his grace? What do we do with our God who promises that his grace is sufficient to cover *all* sin, even sin that seems inhumane at its basest level? Further, how do we *explain* this kind of love and this kind of grace that literally has no bounds, no limits? Can there truly be no thought or act that can trump God's forgiveness?

The answer lies in telling our story. The piercing truth is that all sin is heinous to God. God does not look on murder and treat it as lightly as gossip. God rather, looks on gossip and treats it as horrific and as worthy of eternal punishment as murder. Christ died for all sin and our story lies in the fact that God forgave us of *our* sin. Once we realize that our story of forgiveness is as profound as God's grace being available even to a man like Hitler, we come to realize that we don't just have *a* story to tell but we have *the* story that we *must* tell.

Grace for Me, Justice for You

Funny, isn't it, how we accept grace for ourselves and demand justice for others. For example, when you get stopped for speeding and you see the police officer in your rear-view mirror coming toward your car and motioning you to roll your window down, the last thing to come from your mouth is, "Thank you so much for stopping me! I was speeding and I deserve a ticket. You are doing an excellent job monitoring the street!"

No. You are looking for some mercy.

"Officer I had no idea I was speeding. I'm so sorry. Can you let me go just this once?"

Yet when you see someone else stopped for speeding, as you drive by you think, "It's about time they started monitoring this street (the same street you were stopped on weeks before) for speeders. I hope they catch a bunch of them today."

We all have a breaking point when it comes to what we

deem to be forgivable sin. Very rarely do we apply it to our own circumstances, but for most of us it is well defined for others. We can't believe for a moment that God could or would forgive men such as Hitler, Ted Bundy or Saddam Hussein. Our forgiveness meter is not built to go that high. We cannot conceive of a forgiveness meter that has the potential to *measure* such abomination let alone forgive it. Yet, that is exactly what God offers to each one of us. We are all measured against the perfect sinless life of Jesus and found wanting. We are then forgiven according to the same perfection we are measured against.

WE MUST SHARE ALL OF THE GOOD NEWS; NOT JUST THAT GOD CAN KEEP THEM OUT OF HELL, BUT THAT THEY ARE ABLE TO CLAIM THEIR PLACE IN HEAVEN.

Mercy vs. Grace

We have been given the opportunity to offer the most profound gift in all of creation for all of eternity. Yet we are sometimes compelled to lessen the grandeur of this gift for fear people won't believe it. We tell people they can be saved from their sins if they simply chant to an invisible God. Instead, we should explain the eternal relationship that God desires to have with them, stressing that it is inherently intimate, undeniably eternal and illogically unconditional. God wants them to know that he is not just their "Get Out of Hell Free" card, but that he is their Hope and Peace and Provider and Encourager and Defender and Friend and King and Confidant and Teacher and Supporter! He wants them to know that he will never leave them and he will never forsake them (Deuteronomy 31:6). He desires that they come to understand that he is God and they are not and that he wants to enrich their lives while they are still on earth. At the same time he wants to assure them of the house he has built for them in eternity. He desires them to know that their salvation, their very inheritance as children of God, is waiting for them in heaven and they are unable to damage or lose their inheritance by action or inaction, sinful indulgence or saintly deeds.

We must tell them that they matter to God because God has deemed them important and worthy of his ultimate sacrifice. We must share all of the Good News; not just that God can keep them out of hell, but that they are able to claim their place in heaven. God is not just a God of mercy who would mercifully grant us reprieve from the burning flames of hell, but he is a God of grace who gladly gives us what we don't deserve—an address in heaven.

A friend told me only days into my newfound relationship with God that God is not only a God of mercy, but he is a God of grace. He went on to tell me a story.

"Let's say you shoplifted something from a store and you were caught. When you went in front of the judge and pleaded your case, you would probably say something like, 'Judge, I never shoplifted before and I'll never shoplift again. Please don't give me any jail time.' In other words, you would beg the judge for mercy.

"In the same way, most of us are concerned with staying out of hell and beg for God's mercy to keep us from that fate. We deserve hell because of our sin but we are counting on God to be *merciful*," he explained.

"Getting a reprieve from hell sure sounds good to me," I said. "I wouldn't look a gift horse in the mouth. I'd run out of the courtroom before the judge changed his mind!"

"I understand that feeling," my friend said, "but here's where the story really gets good."

"Okay, you've hooked me."

"Before you have a chance to run out of the courtroom, hardly believing you're getting away with no jail time, the judge stops you and says, 'I also order that you keep the shirt you shoplifted and pick out five more shirts from the same store at the court's expense. Have a nice day, Mr. Phillips.'"

"Whatever!" I replied with a crinkle in my brow.

"That's what grace is, Todd. Mercy is not getting what you deserve but grace is actually *getting something you don't deserve!* That's one of the best parts of the Good News! Not only does God keep you out of hell, but at the expense of Christ's death on the cross you are also given the grace gift of heaven. More important than his mercy is his unfathomable grace!"

People matter to God so much that he went beyond offering his mercy and extended his gift to include his unfathomable grace. Now that's a message people want to hear!

12

The Priceless Value of One Individual to God

I was a keynote speaker at a national Generation X ministry leaders conference last year and the organizers assigned me a specific topic—"Passionate Community." The entire weekend was about passion—passionate relationships and passionate programs and passionate prayer and on and on and on. I focused my talk on the idea of building passionate relationships.

When I am given a topic and begin to develop the sermon, I often open the dictionary and read the definition of the words in the title I've been given. One of the most compelling word searches I've experienced came from simply looking up the word "passion." From a combined reading of the Merriam-Webster Dictionary (1996) and my American Heritage Dictionary, I found that the word had many uses. The four definitions I focused on are:

1. The sufferings of Christ between the night of the Last Supper and his death
2. The emotions as distinguished from reason
3. Rage, anger, love
4. Object of affection or enthusiasm

I was a bit surprised at the first definition—the sufferings of Christ; not just any of his suffering but the hour of his greatest suffering. The word "passion" encompasses all of the sadness Jesus shared with his disciples at his Last Supper with them; his praying with such agony in the garden of Gethsemane that he sweat blood; the unspeakable pain of the nails piercing his skin on the cross and the suffering of his last cry from the cross, "It is finished!" as he gave up his spirit. Passion equals our Savior's greatest suffering.

The second and third definition seemed reasonable enough. I thought it odd that passion could be defined as both rage and love. At first thought they seemed mutually exclusive, then I remembered hearing once that the opposite of love is not hate—it is indifference.

As I read the fourth definition I became curious. I looked up "enthusiasm" in the same two dictionaries.

"Enthusiasm" comes from Greek and means "to be inspired by God."

Now I knew passion was not only the greatest sufferings of Christ, but passion was also the object of my godly inspiration!

So I looked up "inspire" and found that inspiration was "to be moved or guided by divine influence"!

Even in these dictionaries, when you look up the definition of passion and definitions of the words that define passion, you find God—everywhere! If you search for passion in life you will inevitably find God. If you search for a more intimate relationship with God, from that search, passion will be birthed.

I spoke to a veteran of the annual conference, Chris Eaton, about why he had attended every year for the past eleven years.

He said, "I'm in my late thirties and most of these people are now younger than me. I come to feed off their passion. This place is oozing with passion. I feel I might slip on the floor at any moment from all the passion seeping out of these young leaders."

I laughed.

"Lots of passion," he said, and flailed his arms around gesturing, "everywhere!"

I thought to myself, what in the world *is* oozing out of all of us. I began to listen to conversations around the conference and heard people talking about the passion they have or the passion they desperately want. Others would speak of their passion for God or their passion to reach secular people. Yet, the definition of passion that clearly related to the mission of the church was not to have strong emotion for something, some group or some cause, but was related to suffering and submission—the sufferings of Christ and submission to the influence of God.

So, if passion deals with suffering, then the development of passionate community must necessarily mean that I have to share not only in the sufferings of Christ but also in the sufferings of others. That's a problem for me. I'm an only child and, as many psychologists will tell you, there are many characteristics that are specific to the personalities of most only children. One of these characteristics was being able to play by myself. I became good at playing by myself. I also was very good at going into what I called my "cave" when I didn't want to deal with people.

In light of my background, it seemed absurd for me to speak to a thousand young church leaders from all over the country on the topic of building passionate community. In fact, if you were to ask my wife, Julie, she would admit that developing and nourishing interpersonal relationships is not my strong suit. Yet, it became so abundantly clear why I was chosen (not by those in charge of the conference but by God) to be the man on the stage. I came to understand that God wanted to share with that group of leaders (and you, as you read this) something very special about community from a man, in his weakness, who is desperate to grasp the nature and depth of godly relationships and true community.

As I shoveled my way through the topsoil of this still enigmatic concept of passion, I began to realize that every conversation I heard about passion at the conference had two common themes—passion for the cause or the generation and/or passion for God. Yet, godly passion is focused not on the cause or the group or the event—but it is focused on the individual. The sufferings of Christ rather than the suffering of a people, a single object of enthusiasm rather than simply possessing an enthusiastic disposition—is the core of passion. Passion is about "the one." The word "passion" and the personal nature of its true meaning are at the essence of God's theology.

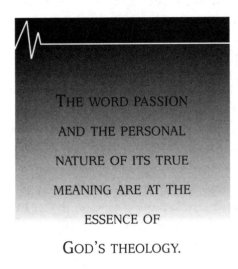

THE WORD PASSION AND THE PERSONAL NATURE OF ITS TRUE MEANING ARE AT THE ESSENCE OF GOD'S THEOLOGY.

Honesty dictates that we admit that having passion for an event or a group or a cause is in numerous ways easier than sharing in the sufferings and diving into the misery and hopelessness of the individual. Yet, that is where passion is found.

A Troubling Passage of Scripture

A verse in the Bible that was extremely confusing to me until very recently was Luke 15. In this chapter there are three stories. One story is of a shepherd who, realizing that one sheep had gone astray, left the ninety-nine sheep in the flock to attempt to find the one that was lost.

In fact, as Jesus is telling the story, he acts as if everyone hearing him speaking would obviously leave the ninety-nine and go after the one: "Suppose one of you has a hundred sheep and loses one of them. Does he not leave the ninety-nine in the open country and go after the lost sheep until he finds it?" (Luke 15:4) The story hinges on the supposition that it is completely normal to respond in this way. The text even goes so far as to imply that it would be abnormal to do otherwise.

Summary time—Here you have a supposedly dedicated shepherd tending to his flock and one, just one, sheep wanders off into a wilderness full of wolves and other menacing creatures. Remember, the shepherd has effectively corralled ninety-nine of the sheep in his care, keeping them from danger.

I was in Sunday school one morning listening to this story for the first time, astonished that everyone in the class seemed to be tracking with the logic of the story. The consensus seemed to be that it was the normal and prudent thing to do for the shepherd to leave the ninety-nine sheep and head off into the wilderness searching for this one not too intelligent sheep that wandered off on its own.

I put my hand up.

"Why in the world does everybody applaud this shepherd for leaving ninety-nine sheep who are safe in his care to search for one sheep who very likely has already been killed? The potential then is that the lost sheep is dead, the shepherd loses his way and starves to death in the wilderness while wolves also eat the ninety-nine sheep which were safe under the watch-care of the now dead shepherd. Now everybody's dead."

"Yes, Todd," the teacher said in a reassuring but slightly patronizing fashion. "But we haven't finished the story. You'll get the point of the story here in just a minute."

"I get the point of the story and it's a good point but it's a bad example."

I had already jumped ahead a few verses and knew the end of the story.

"It's a fairy tale. This isn't real life. In this story he finds the lost sheep unharmed. The assumption is that the rest of the flock is okay and then the shepherd has a party when he gets back to town with all his friends because he found his lost sheep."

The teacher, knowing I was a very new Christian, allowed me to express my angst. He hoped, I must assume as I look back on the situation, that something productive would come from the mouth of a spiritual infant. He seemed to be willing to allow me the stage.

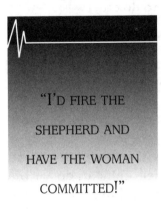

"I'D FIRE THE SHEPHERD AND HAVE THE WOMAN COMMITTED!"

"Then the next example is more ridiculous."

I explained the next story in Luke 15:8–10 about the woman who has ten silver coins and loses one. I looked down at the passage and read part of verse 8,

"'Does she not light a lamp, sweep the house and search carefully until she finds it?' There's that same 'does she not' thing again, as though it's normal to ransack a house to find one coin when you already have nine in the hand. Then she does the same thing that the shepherd did. She gets all her friends together for a party at her house and for what reason? 'Rejoice with me; I have found my lost coin.' What's up with that?"

I'm thinking to myself, "I'd fire the shepherd and have the woman committed!"

The teacher remained calm.

"Todd, you make a great point and several very insightful observations, but the focus is not on the details of the story. The focus, what God is trying to teach us, is the moral of the story—

each and every one of us is priceless to God and that if even one of us repents, all of heaven has a party! After all," he reminded me, "these stories assure us that there was a huge angelic party going on just months ago when you gave your life to Jesus, Todd. That's what God wants you to know from these stories."

He gave me a reassuring smile and then turned back to his notes and continued with the discussion among the members of the class until class time ended. I didn't speak another word for the rest of class that day. Something was bothering me about the two stories. Something hit me wrong when the teacher claimed that the moral was inherently more important than the details of the story that lead us to the moral.

A perfect God wrote, through the hands of many servants throughout history, the words in the Bible. Of all the eternal knowledge God possesses he chose in his infinite wisdom to leave us with only somewhere in the neighborhood of a thousand pages of text. The Bible itself claims that there would not be room in the whole world for the books that would be written just to give an account of the miracles of Jesus, let alone his teachings, Paul's letters, and the entire Old Testament.

In his perfection then, God the all-knowing, all-seeing Creator of everything compiles what we now know as the Bible. We are then to surmise that the events and stories that he sovereignly chose to leave with us to reveal his character, his interaction throughout history with mankind and his ultimate sacrifice of Jesus, his only Son, as payment for the forgiveness of our sins, are *not* to be diligently studied? We are to assume that the story and its details do not have the same God-given ability to impart wisdom, as does the moral itself?

No. There was something there to be gleaned from the story itself besides its moral. The Bible itself has infinite depth, and God, according to his own character, would not tell a story just to provide a moral. If this were his ultimate purpose the Bible would be nothing more than an expanded list of proverbs. I have concluded in my relatively short time as a preacher and teacher of the Word, that I could teach weekly from any passage of Scripture for an indefinite period of time without repeating an illustration, point or application. God would reveal fresh truth hidden within the words waiting to be birthed at his allotted time for those who would hear.

God's Word is a deep well of eternal wisdom whose fathoms are numbered greater than the sands on all the shores of every sea. No human could fashion a machine to reach its depths.

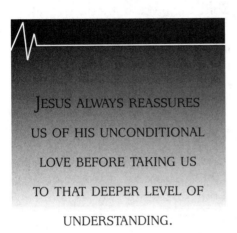

JESUS ALWAYS REASSURES US OF HIS UNCONDITIONAL LOVE BEFORE TAKING US TO THAT DEEPER LEVEL OF UNDERSTANDING.

Computers have enabled us to create software to condense our research time of given passages only to remind us that the more we discover about his Word the more we realize we do not know. There is a strange and wonderful paradox in this experience of untouchable intimacy that we can have with God's Word.

Many times Jesus tells a story in front of the crowd and the crowd does not get the moral. Jesus, though, must even explain to his disciples later in private both the stated moral and the hidden message. The Bible clearly refers to the fact that Jesus spoke in parables so that those who were not meant to understand would be blind to the meaning of the story itself. Time and time again the disciples must come to Jesus privately after his sermon to the masses and ask for an explanation.

As I read and reread these accounts in Luke 15 it became clear that the moral of the story of God's love for me was a wonderful and reassuring truth. However, as Jesus did with the woman caught in adultery, he was expressing his unconditional love for me and of my infinitely priceless value to him before he began to lead me into the depths of the wisdom well.

Here's a quick review of the story about the woman caught in adultery. The religious leaders bring the woman before Jesus and they ask him what they should do with her, because the Scripture says that adultery is punishable by stoning. Jesus says, "If any one of you is without sin, let him be the first to throw a stone at her" (John 8:7). Each of the religious leaders is cut to the core and walks away.

Then Jesus does a remarkable thing. After her accusers are gone he asks her a question.

"Woman, where are they? Has no one condemned you?"

"No one, sir," she said.

"Then neither do I condemn you," Jesus declared. "Go now and leave your life of sin" (John 8:10–11).

The order of his response has forever changed me. He first reassures her of his love for her and his endless wellspring of forgiveness. Only then, after he has expressed his unconditional love does he instruct her to go and sin no more. Jesus always reassures us of his unconditional love before taking us to that deeper level of understanding. Not begrudgingly then, but from our gratitude we obey.

The deeper meaning was in the story. The issues I had with the decisions of both the shepherd and the woman searching for her coin led to a deeper truth, a deeper issue in my own heart that I would find personally disturbing. The moral itself reveals that God is the shepherd who seeks out his lost sheep and he is also the woman who desperately searches until she finds her lost coin. Of course, then, we can understand Jesus when he repeatedly uses the phrase "does he/she not ... " because we have no doubt that God would act in the way described in the parable. Yet, the stories were of a shepherd and a woman acting in like manner to that of God.

The troubling truth was that we have been called, we have been commanded, to leave the ninety-nine to find the one. The

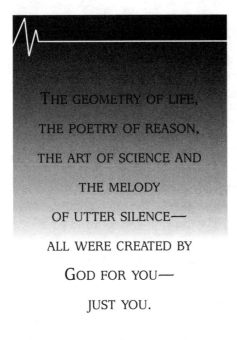

THE GEOMETRY OF LIFE,

THE POETRY OF REASON,

THE ART OF SCIENCE AND

THE MELODY

OF UTTER SILENCE—

ALL WERE CREATED BY

GOD FOR YOU—

JUST YOU.

expectation of sacrifice was the burden that over-took me. I felt smothered by the idea that Nouwen's experience with the severely disabled (chapter 10) was expected of every man! Not that we should all quit our jobs, give away all our money and live on the campus of an asylum wiping the bedpans of others, but that we, or more to the point, *I* am called to value the individual over the crowd and consider sacrifice on behalf of a stranger to be its own reward, one worth pursuing with vigor.

Standing Before a Crowd of Leaders

So, there I was, standing before a crowd of leaders. These young men and women were there, for the most part, because they had built or were in the pursuit of building large gatherings of young adults for weekly worship all around the United States. The unspoken theme was "the bigger the better." As a matter of fact, I was selected to speak to that group on that day, precisely because I was involved in building massive weekly singles events numbering in the hundreds or thousands in both Austin and San Antonio, Texas. I was, at the time, also planting a church for young people in Kerrville, Texas, and experiencing unexpected growth in a very small town in a very short time.

The implication was that I was worthy of the stage and stood as an example of Christian leadership for a new generation simply because I knew how to draw a crowd. Then it became crystal clear. The passion that was oozing out of this young gathering of leaders was for the cause, the group, the gathering. Not one conversation was about having passion for "the one."

They were leaning forward expecting to learn the secret of building the event, drawing people to the cause, satisfying the crowd. But I was about to devalue the crowd, devalue the event, call to question the cause. Then at that moment—when many would be desperately trying to rearrange my words, explain away my criticisms, convince themselves that they must have missed some word or phrase that, if heard, would explain away what they thought I was saying—their thoughts would shift from valuing the crowd to valuing the one. If I helped them to achieve this fundamental shift in thinking then they would be forever changed (or I would be dismissed as just another radical who could be dismissed with all those who simply did not agree with their current paradigm).

The value, I asserted, rested in the individual above all, as the greatest creation of God and priced exceedingly and abundantly higher than any event, crowd or cause. Even the grand desire of many to change the world would cease to carry the weight of a feather compared with the mountainous weight and dense thickness of God's love for "the one."

As I asked the leaders in the room that day to hear me out, I will ask you—for whatever reason you have chosen to continue—to read on. Regardless of your still undetermined response to the coming pages, I also want to say this: The geometry of life, the poetry of reason, the art of science and the melody of utter silence—all were created by God for you—just you. All existence, in essence, exists for you, to represent the depth and height and width of God's love for you—"the one" among millions.

Changing the World, One Soul at a Time

How does this all translate to the topic of evangelism? I was driving my car pondering that very question not long after speaking at the conference. The time—4:30 p.m. The place—Austin, Texas. The problem—traffic! My wife will be quick to tell (or warn) you that the discipline of driving has been the one area in my life where I have enjoyed little or no maturity as a Christian. (Needless to say, I don't have a "Jesus Fish" stuck to the back of my car.) I drive as though I am the only person on the road.

As traffic became worse by the minute, I attempted to stem my natural reactions to the ever more frequent driving faux pas of others on the road by singing along with a worship CD. As I was "doing church" in my car I noticed a young man tailgating me. If there's one thing I really can't stand, it's tailgaters. So, as he inched closer (and as I was singing along to the chorus of "Lord I Lift Your Name on High") I took my foot off the gas and tapped my brakes several times. "Take that!" I said as I looked for his reaction in my rearview mirror. With a startled look, he backed off.

Moments later a car nearly took off my front right bumper while merging into my lane, no blinker, no hand waving apologetically. I imagined following that man home, waiting for him to park, leaning through his rolled-down window and pulling his blinker switch completely off from the steering column and saying with a smile, "Obviously you don't need this!"

Right in the middle of my rather satisfying daydream, the entire scene disappeared from my mind and I remembered a verse that I had been studying a few nights before,

> When [Jesus] saw the crowds, *he had compassion on them*, because they were harassed and helpless, like sheep without a shepherd (Matthew 9:36).

I reflected on my circumstances, my selfishness, and on my lack of compassion for the people on the road around me. It was as if God were telling me, "You need to start seeing people the way that I see people! You see people with an apathetic heart. I see people and feel compassion. Are you my servant? Do you love me? Then feed my sheep rather than leaving them hungry."

I looked to my right and saw a young lady driving alone in her car with a dazed look on her face. I saw her—differently. I imagined that she was driving home from a job where she was sexually harassed daily, but felt powerless to do anything because she needed the money to support her five-year-old son. I looked to my left and spied a man lifting his lighter to light his cigarette, windows closed and smoke engulfing the cabin from other cigarettes lit, smoked, and snuffed out. I imagined he was making a choice that he had made nearly every day for the past several years to stop off at the local strip club and have a few martinis to numb his senses before driving home to fight with his wife again until they retired for the night.

My imagination drew me into the many lives of those around me in traffic that day and one formerly comatose emotion rushed to the surface near the end of my travels—compassion. God took the one activity (driving) that I had yet to hand over to him and used it to help me finally see people the way God sees people—like sheep without a shepherd.

God's view of the individual translates into our perspective on evangelism in this way—as believers, our love for people (plural) must be transformed into the active, participatory love of the *individuals* around us. If God values the individual above all, then we must value the individual, all individuals, in the same way. We, then, cannot limit our prayers for God to fashion opportunities for us to share God's grace with just our brother or our best friend. We must abandon our own biases and pray that God would help us see our friends and enemies in the same way. Our desire to share our faith must be developed to the point where we embrace opportunities to share our faith with whomever God may bring.

Many people will tell me of their vigilant prayers for the salvation of their friend or family member but rarely do I hear of people praying for their inconsiderate and rude coworker or for their ex-wife. I said rarely. It does happen, but it is not the norm. Many of us want to customize our witnessing opportunities and share with those people who are important to us instead of those whom God deems worthy of our witness.

Yet, as children of God we do not have that luxury. We may choose to continue praying only for our friends and family but cannot blame God for the "lostness" of those for whom we pray. He may never give us the opportunity to share our faith with our friends and family. Why? For starters, he knows us and he knows us better than we know ourselves. In his infinite wisdom he may determine that, for a myriad of reasons that only he can understand, we will never be added to the witness list of many of our friends and family members. Yet, he may have had us on the witness list of our rude coworker for years! We cannot blame God for the lack of opportunities to share our faith if we ourselves are turning a blind eye to the myriad of evangelistic opportunities afforded us by God through those others in our lives for whom we *choose* not to share. Everyone is priceless to God, but, and more importantly, every ONE is priceless to God. Ours is a life of submission to God's plan and he chooses how our lives mix with those around us. This mixture, his mixture, is what brings hope to the hopeless and faith to the faithless.

13
Getting Practical: What Is the Result of Our Misunderstanding?

Many in the church today see evangelism as the responsibility of vocational ministers and missionaries rather than an opportunity for every believer to experience complete joy (1 John 1:4). Many in the church have wrongly tied evangelism to a church event rather than an intricate part of the lifestyle of every believer. Many in the church believe evangelism to be about the crowd rather than about the individual. We have addressed these issues in previous chapters, but before we go on to addressing how to share our faith, let's look at some of the results of our skewed perspectives on evangelism. They are staggering.

Thirty years ago America was considered, and rightly so, the world's top missionary-sending country. Now, according to some, we are the third largest mission field in the world! Christians from all over the world perceive the United States of America as the land with the most opportunity—*for conversions!*

Impossible as this may sound, it is true. America is now a post-Christian culture, meaning that the generations we are raising up who are in their teens and twenties do not, for the most part, believe in the God of Abraham, Isaac, and Jacob. They may have heard the story of Jesus but do not hold to the idea that Jesus is the only way to heaven, nor do they believe he was God in human form. Among those who have attended church in the past, many have turned their backs on the faith of their fathers only to replace it with one of dozens of humanistic, New Age religions. These religions, these gods, are chosen by man rather than man being chosen by God. Both gods and doctrines are custom made to fit the current trends and cultural norms of these generations so they will not have to change their lifestyles to fit into their chosen religion. On the contrary, their chosen religion actually affirms their existential choices.

Spirituality or Religion?

The definition of the word *religion* itself has become enigmatic at best. *Spirituality* has replaced *religion* as the buzzword for the youth of this new millennium. Young people no longer seek pastors and priests for wise counsel. Instead, they seek knowledge from internet sites and books written by self-help gurus and New Age philosophers as sources for insight, inspiration and doctrines for living. Whether or not this tide can be stemmed is debatable, but we must acknowledge this trend

> CHRISTIANS FROM ALL OVER THE WORLD PERCEIVE THE UNITED STATES OF AMERICA AS THE LAND WITH THE MOST OPPORTUNITY— FOR CONVERSIONS!

and address it as a contemporary crisis for the church at large. This reality is symptomatic of a generation that sees the church as an increasingly irrelevant source for answers to life's problems. If we don't address this issue in a timely fashion we will be forced to accept the world's perception that the church is irrelevant. And that perception will become reality for generations to come.

To what do we attribute the increasing age of the average church attendee? Why are nearly 80 percent of all churchgoers over thirty-four? Should we be concerned that one-third of church attendees are over fifty-three? (www.barna.org, research archives) Where are the leaders of tomorrow's church? They are not seeking direction from the church today. They spend more time in Barnes and Noble bookstores than church pews. They are the consumers of the new religions and spirituality. They hunger for something, and not knowing how to satisfy their appetite, they search in all the wrong places.

Over the past several years I have had my eye on weekly best-seller lists such as the New York Times Best-Seller List. Some of the best-selling authors over the past four or five years might astound the average church attendee. For example, Deepak Chopra, a New Age self-help guru, has over thirty books and countless seminar tapes to his credit. The title of

... THEY ALLOW THESE BASTARDIZED FORMS OF RELIGION TO INFILTRATE THEIR HEARTS AND MINDS AND COMMINGLE WITH THE BIBLICAL THEOLOGY THEY ARE TAUGHT FROM THE PULPITS OF THEIR CHURCHES.

one of his most popular books is *How to Know God*. I have talked to many Christians who have no idea that Chopra's New Age philosophy is in stark contrast to biblical teaching. They find themselves perusing the religion section at a bookstore, see a book that is titled *How to Know God* and buy it on the spot. With much of today's churchgoing community largely biblically illiterate—at least to the point of being unable to discern the sometimes subtle shifts in theology propagandized by men such as Chopra—they allow these bastardized forms of religion to infiltrate their hearts and minds and commingle with the biblical theology they are taught from the pulpits of their churches.

Adding to the destructive forces of the false teachings of wolves in sheep's clothing such as Chopra, we have men such as Neale Donald Walsh who claim to have been given new revelations directly from God. He claims to have been chosen to bless us "less fortunate" souls who do not have the number to God's private line, by penning these conversations in a series of books starting with the title *Conversations with God: An Uncommon Dialogue*. Not only does this fly in the face of all biblical teaching regarding the sanctity and trustworthiness of the canonized Bible as the only source of written teaching from God, but the author has the audacity to use, as does Chopra, an ever so slightly altered mirror of biblical truth as its foundation. To the reader not well versed in biblical teaching these words seem not only harmless but empowering, so that some would argue naively that these men are teachers of biblical truth. They are not.

Then of course there is the man among men in the myriad of man-conceived religions, none other than the Dalai Lama himself. Books titled *How to Practice: The Way to a Meaningful Life* and *An Open Heart: Practicing Compassion in Everyday Life* tantalize those seeking spirituality in their lives. They capture the hearts of infant Christians who have little if any ability to differentiate a hollow, worldly philosophy from the genuine offer of a personal and everlasting relationship with God himself offered in the Bible.

The teachings of these philosophers and self-professed prophets of God fly in the face of Christianity. God calls for his children, those who have acknowledged Jesus as their personal Lord and Savior, to surrender not just their lives but also their lifestyles to his will. God demands that our hearts be given to him, but he demands the rest of our bodies as well. The diverse marketplace of religions available today only ask their followers to abide by, or at least contemplate the validity of the intellectual and/or philosophical credo of their chosen faith.

Chopra falsely calls for the recognition of the god in each of us. Conversely, the one true God rightly and justly calls us to bow before his majesty, to contemplate and acknowledge daily that he is God and we are not. Man's arrogance and pride has always been one of the greatest examples of our need for a savior. To Chopra, as well as to each one of us who would suggest in our arrogance that we are our own gods, God would pose these questions as he did to Job thousands of years ago:

> Then the LORD answered Job from the whirlwind: "Who is this that questions my wisdom with such ignorant words? Brace yourself, because I have some questions for you, and you must answer them.
>
> "Where were you when I laid the foundations of the earth? Tell me, if you know so much. Do you know how its dimensions were determined and who did the surveying? ... Do you know where the gates of death are located? Have you seen the gates of utter gloom? Do you realize the extent of the earth? Tell me about it if you know!
>
> "Where does the light come from, and where does the darkness go? Can you take it to its home? Do you know how to get there? But of course you know all this!

For you were born before it was all created, and you are so very experienced! ...

"Can you hold back the movements of the stars? Are you able to restrain the Pleiades or Orion? Can you ensure the proper sequence of the seasons or guide the constellation of the Bear with her cubs across the heavens? Do you know the laws of the universe and how God rules the earth?

"Can you shout to the clouds and make it rain? Can you make lightning appear and cause it to strike as you direct it? Who gives intuition and instinct? Who is wise enough to count all the clouds? Who can tilt the water jars of heaven, turning the dry dust to clumps of mud?

"Can you stalk prey for a lioness and satisfy the young lions' appetites as they lie in their dens or crouch in the thicket? Who provides food for the ravens when their young cry out to God as they wander about in hunger?" (Job 38:1–5, 17–21, 31–41 NLT)

Walsh, as with Chopra, has his own philosophy that he claims to have received from the very person of God. He would have us believe his horrifically flawed premise that God himself has established many roads to heaven and man is free to choose his path. Yet the true God who literally spoke the entire universe into existence makes clear that his Son, Jesus, is the only way to forgiveness and everlasting life (John 14:6).

The Dalai Lama would have us all attempt in vain to earn our way to Nirvana by living many lives over and over until we get it right. All the while, the one true God, who knows exactly how many grains of sand are on the beaches of the world, says there is no man who is righteous, not even one who could ever be perfect, sinless, spotless enough to earn his way to heaven (Romans 3:23).

The Bible warns with sharp words and piercing clarity that the solution to the marred condition of mankind is not in the words of its philosophers or the theorems of its scientists or the rhetoric of its scholars and debaters. No. The solution is the cross of Christ:

I know very well how foolish the message of the cross sounds to those who are on the road to destruction. But we who are being saved recognize this message as the very power of God. As the Scriptures say,

"I will destroy human wisdom and discard their most brilliant ideas."

So where does this leave the philosophers, the scholars,

> THE CROSS OF JESUS CHRIST IS STILL THE ONLY ANSWER FOR THE MARRED CONDITION OF MANKIND AND THE CROSS STILL "SOUNDS FOOLISH" TO THOSE WHO ARE ON THE ROAD TO DESTRUCTION.

and the world's brilliant debaters? God has made them all look foolish and has shown their wisdom to be useless nonsense. Since God in his wisdom saw to it that the world would never find him through human wisdom, he has used our foolish preaching to save all who believe. God's way seems foolish to the Jews because they want a sign from heaven to prove it is true. And it is foolish to the Greeks because they believe only what agrees with their own wisdom. So when we preach that Christ was crucified, the Jews are offended and the Gentiles say it's all nonsense. But to those called by God to salvation, both Jews and Gentiles, Christ is the mighty power of God and the wonderful wisdom of

God. This "foolish" plan of God is far wiser than the wisest of human plans, and God's weakness is far stronger than the greatest of human strength.

Remember, dear brothers and sisters, that few of you were wise in the world's eyes, or powerful, or wealthy when God called you. Instead, God deliberately chose things the world considers foolish in order to shame those who think they are wise. And he chose those who are powerless to shame those who are powerful. God chose things despised by the world, things counted as nothing at all, and used them to bring to nothing what the world considers important, so that no one can ever boast in the presence of God. God alone made it possible for you to be in Christ Jesus. For our benefit God made Christ to be wisdom itself. He is the one who made us acceptable to God. He made us pure and holy, and he gave himself to purchase our freedom. As the Scriptures say, "The person who wishes to boast should boast only of what the Lord has done" (1 Corinthians 1:18–31 NLT).

The scholars, debaters, philosophers, self-help experts, talk-show hosts, motivational speakers, and even some of the religious leaders of our time are no different than those whom Paul spoke out against in his day. Our condition is the same as those in Corinth to whom Paul wrote his impassioned letter. The cross of Jesus Christ is still the only answer for the marred condition of mankind and the cross still "sounds foolish" to those who are on the road to destruction.

Sharing a Clear Message

We, however, must take it upon ourselves to convey this message effectively to our generation. We must first want to convey this message of hope, but I believe, again, that if you have come this far with me you now desire to be an effective communicator of the Good News. You now see the opportunity that lies ahead, not only for those with whom you share the Gospel but also for you, through God's promise of complete joy! Yet, against the backdrop of so many religions and philosophers who package their stories so well, how can we possibly compete?

Let me put your mind at ease. There is no competition. I've read the end of the Bible and we do win! In fact, God tells us in his Word that if we do nothing, sit silent and refuse to enter the playing field, then the rocks will literally cry out the name and the majesty of Jesus. A day is coming when every knee will bow and every tongue will confess the name of Jesus, the Ruler of the Universe and Lord of All (Philippians 2:10–11).

Yet, with the times as they are and the buffet of religions available to man, some churches and denominations have chosen to change the message rather than the method in order to attempt to seem more relevant to people in our time. In doing so they fall into the same trap as every generation before. They take the message fashioned by the same God who created the universe and hears the prayers of billions of people and replace it with a hollow, lifeless, hopeless message created by man. Paul dealt with the same problem and responded to it directly, to several churches in his day. He warned them not to listen to those who preached "another Jesus" (2 Corinthians 11).

So, in an ironic twist, mankind continues to create religions for itself in a vain attempt to deal with the human condition, when all the while God has already offered us an eternal relationship with himself through his Son, Jesus Christ.

Now, here comes another twist.

God calls for those who would follow him to deny themselves, take up their cross and follow him (Mark 8:34). He does not ask this of us in return for an eternal relationship with him. He gives eternity as a free, unmerited, undeserved, unearned gift for anyone who would call on the name of the Lord: a gift from God through the death, burial and resurrection of his Son, Jesus. Yet, every other religion and philosophy claims to impart the instructions on how to earn one's passage to heaven or to ascend to some mode of perfection. Some religions are even so bold as to claim to show us how to become a god. They claim to show us how to earn eternity, perfection, or godhood. They show us what they claim we must do for God. In stark contrast, Christianity is the only religion that speaks not of what we must do for God but of what God has already done for us through Jesus Christ. Our message is different. Our message is truth. Our message offers true hope to the hopeless and life to the lifeless.

14
Be Loyal No Matter What!

My story begins in Denver, Colorado, in January 1994. I was living out of wedlock with a young woman I'll call Brooke. We rented a condo in a suburb just west of Denver. I was chasing the dollar religiously and that pursuit landed me in Denver with that woman at that time. Brooke was a beautiful and street-smart young woman who, at the ripe old age of twenty-one, had, with my urging, successfully blueprinted the entire operation of a strip club she managed in Austin, Texas. We moved to Denver to open one of these "sexually oriented businesses," as it was termed by the Denver Vice Squad. At the time, the Denver laws pertaining to these types of businesses were less strict than in some other major cities such as Houston, Texas, where, after two long years, we were unsuccessful at our attempts to open a club.

My job was to find the seed money and Brooke's job was to manage the club. I did my part and she successfully opened the club in downtown Denver in the summer of 1993. Other than some major hurdles we encountered in the first few months, we were off and running. I called a friend back in Austin to offer him a piece of the pie if he would move up to Denver and help us open two more clubs, one in Albuquerque, New Mexico, and one in Phoenix, Arizona. He agreed and within two weeks he had moved into the extra bedroom of our condominium. I was beginning to realize my dream of being wealthy and controlling my own life. I was accumulating at least the beginning of what I had spent the past twelve years of my life pursuing—money.

In the middle of these events I received one very important phone call from my mother. She called on a regular basis to express her concern at the choices I was making. She would ask me, "How did my son, who was president of his high school student council, end up opening strip clubs?" As you can imagine, I didn't welcome these calls and usually hung up on her fairly soon after I picked up the phone. This particular call was different, though. Mom seemed to be in a good mood even after I said my usual, "Oh, it's you. What do you want?"

"I ran into an old friend of yours at a Ricky Trevino concert here in Austin last night."

"Mom, can't you just give me the whole story without these conversational pauses where I'm supposed to say 'Who?'"

"Well, I saw Todd Riddle." I hadn't heard that name in five or six years. Todd was a guy I'd met in my drug days at Texas Tech University back in the late eighties. He and I were involved in starting an organization at Texas Tech called the Young Entrepreneur Society (Y.E.S.). This is the same guy who shared my excitement for cocaine. He was a professional manipulator and con artist like me. I couldn't help but be curious about where he was and what he was doing now.

"I haven't heard that name in a while."

"You won't believe what he's doing now!" Mom said. I stayed quiet. I refused to get caught up in the back-and-forth, question-and-answer dialogue on which my mother was insisting. I stayed quiet knowing she wouldn't be able to hold her tongue.

"He's a Gospel singer!" she said. "He travels around and sings at churches about Jesus. He has a CD out. I heard it on the speakers in the auditorium during intermission at the concert!"

As I processed the information I'd just heard, it simply would not marry with the current database of information I had on Riddle from our time together half a decade earlier.

"That's ... great, Mom. Anything else you wanted to tell me? I've got to go."

"That's it. I just thought you'd be interested in hearing what Todd Riddle was up to now."

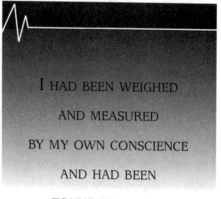

I HAD BEEN WEIGHED

AND MEASURED

BY MY OWN CONSCIENCE

AND HAD BEEN

FOUND WANTING.

I hung up the phone and tried to put the conversation out of my mind, but I couldn't. There was no way that the Todd Riddle I knew could be singing Gospel music anywhere for any reason, except ... "That's what he's doing!" I said to myself. "This is just another money-making project! He's pulled another fast one!" I told myself this was the only viable option. Yet, the potential reality of Todd Riddle singing Gospel, even for profit, was too much for my mind to wrap around.

A few days later I woke up and went into the bathroom to splash some water on my face. As I dried my face off with a towel I looked in the mirror and saw a few drops of water streaming down from my hairline and settling on my eyebrow. I took a deep breath, and for some unknown reason I looked at my reflection and said to myself, "If you keep on doing what you're doing in this business—in this relationship—you're going to feel even more stupid and empty than you do now."

I was caught in an "ah-ha" moment and I wanted to run but I couldn't move. I stared at my reflection; an empty shell that was once Todd Phillips. An empty shell pursuing money and success and power, only to find that just glimpses of these pursuits were enough to bring an overwhelming sense of emptiness and lack of meaningful purpose to my being. I was empty. I had been weighed and measured by my own conscience and had been found wanting.

I felt as if I would have to physically turn my head with my own hand to pull myself from this painful experience.

I forced my head down into the sink below me, my breath echoing in the basin.

"I've made my bed," I said with a sense of utter defeat and walked out of the bathroom trying to forget my reflection, trying to forget my conversation with my mother, trying to refuse the feeling of utter loneliness and emptiness that was with me every waking moment, but I was able to forget nothing.

The rest of the day was uneventful and though my goal was always to fall asleep early and get up late, thinking I should pass as much of my time unconscious as I could, I once again found myself wide awake at two in the morning.

The next night was again filled with maddening wakefulness. Every minute was marked by the slight change in pitch of the buzz of the electrical current in the alarm clock less than a foot from my ear. After some time I found I could actually gauge the exact moment the clock would turn to the next minute. This wasn't healthy. I pulled myself out of bed, leaving Brooke asleep, and went quietly downstairs to make a phone call. Two days now since I first felt the void between me and my own reflection in the mirror, and nearly a week buffered me from my conversation with my mom, but time hadn't lessened their effects. I simply had to call Todd Riddle. I had to discount the potential—however unlikely—that Todd was now a Christian singer. I had to lay to rest the possibility that someone like Todd Riddle—like me—could change so drastically. I picked up the phone and called information.

"Yeah, Austin, Texas, number for a Todd Riddle."

After a short pause, "Please hold for that number," said the operator before connecting me to the recording of Todd's phone number. I pushed the flash button on my phone to get a dial tone and called the number.

The phone rang only once and, after a significant number of bumping sounds as if the phone were being dragged by the cord from the base unit to Todd's ear, I heard, "Mmmm ... Todd."

"Hey, um, Todd, this is Todd ... "

"Phillips?" he said as he made every effort to stay conscious.

"Yeah, it's Todd Phillips. What are you doing?"

"I'm sleeping! It's after two in the morning."

I didn't acknowledge his sarcastic remark. I couldn't hold inside the question that had kept me up each night for the past week. I had no idea that Todd's answer would spark a curiosity in me that would result in my introduction to Jesus.

"I heard from my mom that you are singing Gospel music now and you have a CD out and everything. So, what's the scam? How much money are you making off this project?" Impatiently, I waited for his response, but his reply didn't match any of the possible answers I had imagined.

"Todd," he said as he stretched and groaned, "it's not like that at all. I *give* those CDs away to people so they can learn more about Jesus."

Nothing in my arsenal of comebacks was appropriate for his reply. I remained silent, confused at what my ears had just heard. His illogical statement kept me on the phone for the next three hours that night. He told me about Jesus and when he asked me questions about my own circumstances I avoided the question or simply hung up on him. Then I called back—collect. I figured if he was going to tell me about Jesus and he believed so much in him then he wouldn't mind footing the bill for the long distance charges.

Night after night for over a month I called him, hung up on him, and called him back several times. I cursed at him, called him a liar, screamed that his Christianity was a joke. Through all of this he kept listening, he kept answering the phone, he continued to accept the charges. His undying loyalty was a character trait he did not possess when I knew him before, and it was such a strong part of who he seemed to be now that I was compelled to keep our dialogue open.

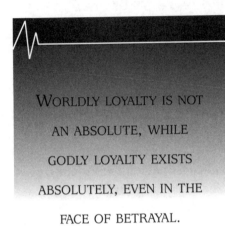

WORLDLY LOYALTY IS NOT AN ABSOLUTE, WHILE GODLY LOYALTY EXISTS ABSOLUTELY, EVEN IN THE FACE OF BETRAYAL.

Loyalty is a key in developing a relationship with anyone, but especially when we as Christians are developing relationships with pre-Christians. The loyalty I speak of here is a godly loyalty that stands in stark contrast to worldly loyalty. Worldly loyalty is not an absolute, while godly loyalty exists absolutely, even in the face of betrayal. Loyalties shift with the tides of power in our world while godly loyalty only strengthens its resolve in the midst of crisis. Loyalties in secular friendships last as long as they are reciprocated. God's version of loyalty is poured out to others with the expectation of nothing in return.

Jesus showed how worldly loyalty could be the most destructive force on earth while godly loyalty can change the world. Judas is the obvious personification of worldly loyalty in the Bible. Although there are many fine examples, Judas stands out. His loyalty to Jesus and his band of disciples was traded in for thirty pieces of silver (Matthew 27:3).

Jesus, conversely, was the obvious personification of godly loyalty. His commitment to his disciples is unmatched by anyone in history before or since. The finest example of his commitment to relationship in spite of utter betrayal was in his relationship to Peter. Peter denied his relationship with Jesus three times to save himself and yet Jesus maintained his loyalty to Peter. It was in this moment of irony, when Jesus repaid betrayal with loyalty, that Peter cemented himself to the side of his friend Jesus, even to the point of death.

As Christians under the power and strength of the Holy Spirit, we have at our disposal the otherworldly ability to tie ourselves to even the most destructive of people and love them in spite of themselves. Yet the church constantly proves itself to be woefully inadequate when it comes to developing loyalty with even those in the church, let alone those outside the faith who desperately want to see something different in us.

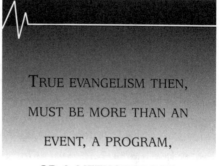

TRUE EVANGELISM THEN, MUST BE MORE THAN AN EVENT, A PROGRAM, OR A METHODOLOGY.

Nietzsche, the great philosopher, said, "I shall not believe in the redeemer of these Christians until they show me they are redeemed."

God's ability to display this kind of commitment to relationships through us is essential to our success at reaching secular people.

Our pre-Christian friends, family members, and enemies are for the most part experiencing the world's philosophy on life, friendship, success, and happiness. We then must show them God's philosophy on these things by building strong, unconditional friendships with them. True evangelism then, must be more than an event, a program or a methodology. Evangelism is lived out most effectively through a process in relationships.

My conversation with Riddle continued each night for almost a month. He would read Scripture to me over the phone, having absolutely no idea that from the very first night I was following along as best I could in my own Bible. When I hung up the phone that first night I went straight to my closet and pulled out a box of books that I had failed to unpack after our move from Houston to Denver. At the bottom of the box was a small Bible I'd received in private elementary school fifteen years earlier. Each night from then on I tried unsuccessfully to follow Riddle's journey through his Bible. I couldn't tell him to slow down for fear he would find out that I was reading the Bible, and I couldn't let him know that. So, being unable to follow him verse by verse, I decided to write down every reference he spoke. My plan each night was to take all the verses he had referred to and, after our final words to one another, attempt to validate (or discredit) what he claimed was from the Bible.

Each night after our conversation I spent the next couple of hours finding each passage and confirming that Todd was giving it to me straight. Every word was there. Nothing was missing. What he was saying was true or at least it was all in the Bible just as he had read it.

One important note is worthy of some discussion. Todd Riddle was completely unaware of the profound effect he was having on me. He tells me now that he thought all of his time reading Scripture to me over the phone was fruitless, and he actually had several Christian friends he called on a regular basis who encouraged him to hang in there with me. If he had only known that I was reading every single verse he quoted. If he had only known that God's Word was piercing my heart. But he didn't. He was forced to have faith in God's ability to soften my heart and believe with conviction that it was happening even when there was absolutely no sign of progress.

Let me encourage you in your efforts to share the Gospel with those around you. You may never see what God is doing in the heart of the person with whom you are building a relationship. You must know, however, that God is working. Your undying loyalty to those with whom you come in contact—especially those who overtly contest the truth you share with them—will go far to validate the kind of unconditional love you claim your God has for them.

15

Listen ... No, I Mean REALLY Listen

Good listeners possess a great earthly power. Power to influence. Power to persuade. Power to effect change. Yet, as a Christian under the influence and inspiration of the Holy Spirit, a man or woman who seeks to be one who truly listens to others possesses a tool with power far beyond the understanding of any man. For in the hands of God any tool or gift or personality trait is being driven by Power Himself.

The Lost Art of Listening

"No one listens to me!" shouted a young lady to her classmates sitting around a study table in the campus library at Texas Tech University.

She stormed out of the library in a huff, tears streaming down her face as her friends looked at each other in disbelief. I was a freshman sitting alone at a table a few feet away watching the scene unfold. The year was 1987, more than fifteen years ago, but I can still remember the hopelessness on her face. Over the previous hour I heard her getting more agitated as she made numerous efforts to elicit some measure of understanding from her girlfriends at the table. I couldn't make out most of the conversation but it was clear that she was concerned, even frantic at times, yet none of the young ladies ever responded. She was looking for just one of them to leave their world and step into hers. She just needed someone, anyone, to lend an ear.

> ... THE ABILITY TO HEAR WITH OUR EARS IS SADLY AND ALL TOO OFTEN MISTAKEN FOR THE ABILITY TO LISTEN WITH OUR HEARTS.

Children have the same complaint about their parents, employees about their bosses, husbands about their wives and wives about their husbands. An epidemic exists in our culture, a disease that affects, by some estimates, over 98 percent of the population. Yet, a strange phenomenon allows this disease to go almost unnoticed. It is a disease of the heart but it is disguised quite effectively by the normal functioning of an altogether different organ—the ear. The vast majority of people are born with the innate ability to hear with their ears. Sound waves enter the ear canal causing the eardrum to beat rhythmically against the tympanic membrane, which causes a series of miraculous events that result in the brain deciphering the vibrations as sound. Yet, the ability to hear with our ears is sadly and all too often mistaken for the ability to listen with our hearts. The vast majority of people do not have the ability to *listen*. What is even more bizarre and ironic is that it seems all of us can identify the disease in those around us but fail to identify it within ourselves.

The resulting chaos that exists in our relationships with one another is devastating. Just as the young woman cried out to her friends in the library that day, many of us have cried out to our parents or a friend or a boss with our face and fists pointed to the sky saying, "No one listens to me!"

Mine was a similar situation. I was one of the masses with this debilitating disease who was unable to diagnose myself, or anyone else for that matter. I woke up each day, put on my mask of choice and paraded out the door to face my audience. It seemed as though they strategically placed themselves in the grocery store, the gas station, and the cars around me at each stoplight. I looked at them and nodded or gestured from behind my mask of manufactured self-confidence, pretending to listen but only hearing their words. Then I would begin to speak, not in response to their words, but from my own quiet desperation to be heard. I would place meaning between the lines of my prose in a vain effort to connect, never realizing that my words were only a buzz or drone in the ears of others.

In the midst of my falling prey to this disease daily, my mother called and gave me the news that Todd Riddle had become a Christian. The words she spoke were a momentary antidote to my affliction. They tore straight to the marrow of my being. I couldn't ignore what I was hearing. My heart listened

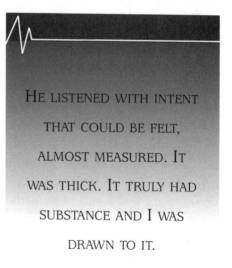

HE LISTENED WITH INTENT THAT COULD BE FELT, ALMOST MEASURED. IT WAS THICK. IT TRULY HAD SUBSTANCE AND I WAS DRAWN TO IT.

to her words about Todd and the words existed so far outside of my realm of understanding that I was compelled to ponder, reflect, even consider their merit instead of brushing them aside. This was not talk of the weather or of taxes or of bad relationships. No, there was much more to this.

Several days later I picked up the phone and began a month-long dialogue with Todd Riddle that was unlike any before or since. He exhibited loyalty, yes, but he exhibited another quality. He listened. He listened to me with all of himself. No one in my memory had ever listened in that way to me. He listened with intent that could be felt, almost measured. It was thick. It truly had substance and I was drawn to it. I know now that it was the Holy Spirit working through Todd Riddle to reach my innermost being, but at the time I was totally unaware of the source. I hungered for such substantive discussion and continued to talk with him night after night.

No Condemnation

Todd listened to my most trivial statements as diligently as he listened to my most pressing questions. What made even more of an impact was his ability to encourage and support me while not encouraging my sin. Todd knew about the sinful life I was leading. He was aware of the pain and confusion and hopelessness that dominated most of my waking thoughts. He was a product of the same choices, the same mistakes, yet he was not the same man I knew years before.

I continued to pour out to Todd because I knew with certainty that I was pouring into a cup that would hold the mass of my misery. He received my words and the hidden meaning between the lines and behind the words. He even seemed to share in the emotions that came with them. Yet, he continued to listen.

I didn't realize any of what was happening at the time, nor could I have described any of it with clarity as I can now. For now I understand the reason I stayed on the phone for hours on end, night after night with Todd Riddle. He listened. More than that though, it was God who was listening to me through Todd, and loving me. I never felt berated or condemned as I spoke of my circumstances. I laid my sins out in detail, looking for Todd to shrink back from his position but nothing could thwart the onslaught of love I was receiving from the other end of the line. He simply received it, empathized with the situation and then offered hope in Jesus.

As Christians many times we are so quick to tell our stories, speak of our blessings, talk of God's love, never realizing that a man or woman who has never known such love simply cannot or will not accept what they are hearing. I've heard this juxtaposition compared with the futility of describing the color green to a man who has been blind from birth. We

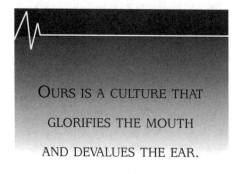

OURS IS A CULTURE THAT GLORIFIES THE MOUTH AND DEVALUES THE EAR.

tell a story of hope and forgiveness. We paint a fantastic scene on the canvas of our hearts with a kaleidoscope of colors, yet they can see nothing of our masterpiece from the darkness. Therefore, we must be willing to dive into other people's misery. To know where to dive, we must be quick to listen to their complaints and concerns and slow to speak. Ours is a culture that glorifies the mouth and devalues the ear. Therefore, a believer who defies the cultural norm and chooses instead to listen is of great use to God.

Are you quick to speak? Are you quick to pull out an evangelistic tract at the drop of a hat? Those around you may applaud your evangelistic zeal, but I would caution you. You must first attempt to gauge your friend's misery factor. You must enter his world and discover his hopelessness quotient.

You must know what he is going through at the deepest levels of his being rather than spout trite and, more often than not, useless answers from the latest book on countering secular arguments against Christianity or some similar publication that trivializes the severity and complexity of life's problems. I have on many occasions heard believers respond to the deep issues of a pre-Christian by saying, "God works in mysterious ways." Whatever!

Please don't think for a moment that I am trying to replace the eternal power of the Holy Spirit with some modern-day psychological quackery. I do know that the Holy Spirit convicts a person of his or her sins and draws that same person to God. I am fully aware that man, in and of himself, can do nothing to save himself or anyone else from the power and the penalty of sin. Nothing is clearer to me than the utter depravity of man. I believe the words of Paul when he explains that the Gospel is foolishness to the world and yet it is the power of God unto salvation for those who are being saved (1 Corinthians 1:18).

Yet, I believe that many Christians today are motivated by Christian zeal rather than God's still, small voice when it comes to witnessing. We accost people with the Gospel and wonder why they don't respond. Our assumption that their hearts are hardened against the Gospel might be inaccurate. They may simply have an aversion to our zeal.

A very good friend of mine is unaware of the damage he causes to his own witness with his religious zeal. I watched as he met someone at a function and the first words that came from his mouth were, "So Keith, do you know Jesus as your Savior?"

Although God uses "cold turkey" (CT) witnessing, we should be motivated by God's leading rather than our own zeal. We should focus most of our energy on aggressive "friendship evangelism" (FE). In FE, friendships become springboards to share the Gospel. We will find people much more open when we approach them as a genuinely caring friend, rather than a religious zealot. In addition, because the person has shared with us many of his or her personal problems, we can show him or her how God can help with a variety of difficulties.

I must emphasize here that we are not to use friendship as a means to an end. Friendship cannot be seen as a tool for winning souls. Friendship must be seen as a reward in itself. We must genuinely seek to develop true friendships with those we meet. Our concern for them must be sincere. If we are not sincere, people will view us like the used car salespeople who pretend to be friendly for the sole purpose of selling a car. We must make it a point to ask God to give us a true love for those we meet.

Friends Are Friends Forever

Ultimately, the friendship itself must be enough for us. God may put us in the life of a lost person just to be his or her friend. There is no expiration date on true friendship. We can't just leave our friend after two years because he is not responding to the Gospel. Ironic as this may sound, the friendship is the cake and our friend's salvation is the icing on the cake. People are not projects—they are people!

I see people and entire churches who track with precision (if not inflation) "their" conversions, genuine or not, as though they had anything to do with the salvation of those people. If we as Christians must keep records of such things, the only statistic even worthy of debate would be the number of lives with whom we *shared* the Gospel or the number of lives with whom we practically shared God's love. God calls us to share—that is all. A 2,000 member church with a $5 million budget cannot convert one soul. So, why do we meticulously record conversions? Do we honestly believe that God needs us to count his conversions? Do we believe that the same God who knows the number of hairs on our head (Matthew 10:30) might miss the birth of even one of his children? I think not.

Too many believers see un-churched people *only* as their

next project rather than a new opportunity to shower someone unconditionally with God's love. We become busy as individuals and congregations patting ourselves on the back for those around us whom *God* saves, rather than finding the next opportunity to pour our lives out to someone while expecting nothing—not praise, not gratitude, not that person's salvation—in return. We have been given the task of loving people and sharing the Gospel. Loving and sharing—we are expected to do no more. Or less!

16

For God's Sake,
Don't Candy-Coat the Gospel

A s Todd Riddle was explaining to me what to expect as a new Christian, he took me to passages in the Bible that may surprise you. In fact, Todd did exactly the opposite of what so many Christians do as they try to share their faith with a nonbeliever.

So many Christians share a message that ignores the tremendous difficulty many new believers find when they come out of a worldly life. Through their newfound faith in Christ they begin to understand that there truly is a better way. Yet, they are not adequately warned of the "storm before the calm" that most new believers experience in the first months or years of their relationship with God.

Riddle made it very clear that I would experience hardship as a new believer and that it would likely be more severe than what I was going through as an unbeliever. If you were listening to the conversation at the time you might have been convinced that Riddle was trying to talk me *out of* becoming a Christian.

He read me passages such as James 1:2–4:

> Consider it pure joy, my brothers, whenever you face trials of many kinds, because you know that the testing of your faith develops perseverance. Perseverance must finish its work so that you may be mature and complete, not lacking anything.

One of his favorites was the ever-popular passage in Romans 7 where Paul says:

> We know that the law is spiritual; but I am unspiritual, sold as a slave to sin. I do not understand what I do. For what I want to do I do not do, but what I hate I do. And if I do what I do not want to do, I agree that the law is good. As it is, it is no longer I myself who do it, but it is sin living in me. I know that nothing good lives in me, that is, in my sinful nature. For I have the desire to do what is good, but I cannot carry it out. For what I do is not the good I want to do; no, the evil I do not want to do—this I keep on doing. Now if I do what I do not want to do, it is no longer I who do it, but it is sin living in me that does it. So I find this law at work: When I want to do good, evil is right there with me. For in my inner being I delight in God's law; but I see another law at work in the members of my body, waging war against the law of my mind and making me a prisoner of the law of sin at work within my members. What a wretched man I am! Who will rescue me from this body of death? Thanks be to God—through Jesus Christ our Lord! So then, I myself in my mind am a slave to God's law, but in the sinful nature a slave to the law of sin (Romans 7:14–25).

Riddle wanted me to understand that the life of a Christian is a life with daily struggles. Riddle was as convinced then as I am now that we have an obligation to those with whom we share the Gospel to prepare them for the almost certain difficulties that come with newfound faith.

I remember well sitting in the pew at Hyde Park Baptist Church in Austin, Texas, only a few weeks after I met Jesus on a hillside in Denver, Colorado. Dr. Ralph Smith, with what I would soon find out was his signature opening comment from the pulpit every Sunday, proclaimed, "This is the day the Lord hath made. Let us rejoice and be glad in it."

I was certain that the Lord had made the day, but I found nothing in my circumstances at that moment to warrant any measure of rejoicing. Later in the sermon he proclaimed, "God loves you!"

"Yeah," I mumbled to myself. "God loves everybody but me."

> WE HAVE AN OBLIGATION TO THOSE WITH WHOM WE SHARE THE GOSPEL TO PREPARE THEM FOR THE ALMOST CERTAIN DIFFICULTIES THAT COME WITH NEWFOUND FAITH.

All hell had broken loose in my life since the night I surrendered myself to Jesus and my honest opinion that morning was, with a friend like God, who needs enemies? Riddle told me things would likely get worse before they got better because God would have to rearrange some things and get rid of other things in my life. I came to expect difficulty to come my way and thought I would be prepared. But I was not at all prepared for the severity.

Yet, the fact that I knew the trials were coming, even though I was not prepared for the severity, was a key to my desire to weather the storm. Riddle's honesty during the process of my salvation formed a very strong opinion in my mind of Todd's—and God's—integrity.

At this point I should mention that, without a doubt the worst day I experienced as a Christian (and there have been some miserable days) is a hundredfold better than the best day (and I had some award-winning days) I ever had as a non-Christian. There simply is no comparison. The end of the story then is that it's all worth it regardless of the hardships, trials, and loss because we all experience these whether we have a relationship with God or not. Trials come to the believer and unbeliever alike but the believer now has God on his side. The new believer can find rest in passages from God's Word such as:

> Consider it pure joy, my brothers, whenever you face trials of many kinds, because you know that the testing of your faith develops perseverance (James 1:2–3).

The unbeliever *cannot*. The new believer knows that there is purpose in his trials:

> In this you greatly rejoice, though now for a little while you may have had to suffer grief in all kinds of trials. These have come so that your faith—of greater worth than gold, which perishes even though refined by fire—may be proved genuine and may result in praise, glory and honor when Jesus Christ is revealed (1 Peter 1:6–7).

The unbeliever *does not* have that assurance.

God Loves Us Too Much to Leave Us the Way We Are

Pre-Christians and new believers must be told, though, why it sometimes gets harder when God takes control of our lives. They must understand that if it gets harder it's not because God hates us, but because he loves us too much to leave us the way we are. This truth is significant.

In Matthew 21 there is a passage known to many as the "Triumphal Entry." As ironic as this may sound, I think this passage is one of the most profound *evangelistic* passages in the Bible. In this passage Jesus is about to enter Jerusalem where in only a matter of days he will allow himself to be put on a cross to die for the sins of the world.

As they approached Jerusalem and came to Bethphage on the Mount of Olives, Jesus sent two disciples, saying to them, "Go to the village ahead of you, and at once you will find a donkey tied there, with her colt by her. Untie them and bring them to me. If anyone says anything to you, tell him that the Lord needs them, and he will send them right away."

This took place to fulfill what was spoken through the prophet: "Say to the Daughter of Zion, 'See, your king comes to you, gentle and riding on a donkey, on a colt, the foal of a donkey.'" The disciples went and did as Jesus had instructed them. They brought the donkey and the colt, placed their cloaks on them, and Jesus sat on them. A very large crowd spread their cloaks on the road, while others cut branches from the trees and spread them on the road. The crowds that went ahead of him and those that followed shouted, "Hosanna to the Son of David! Blessed is he who comes in the name of the Lord! Hosanna in the highest!"

When Jesus entered Jerusalem, the whole city was stirred and asked, "Who is this?" The crowds answered, "This is Jesus, the prophet from Nazareth in Galilee."

Jesus entered the temple area and drove out all who were buying and selling there. He overturned the tables of the money changers and the benches of those selling doves. "It is written," he said to them, "My house will be called a house of prayer, but you are making it a 'den of robbers'" (Matthew 21:1–13).

This passage sums up in profound detail exactly what happens when God takes control of the life of a new believer. This passage, in my humble opinion, should be printed on the back cover of every evangelistic tract. When a believer memorizes the "Roman Road," the four passages in Romans that sum up the good news for a nonbeliever, they should also memorize this passage!

Let me explain.

Since his birth, Jesus had been traveling toward Jerusalem for the events of the coming week. He knew what awaited him in Jerusalem—an angry mob that would choose a convicted murderer over him, a religious oligarchy that saw him as a threat to their power base, a thief who would hang on a cross beside him pleading for forgiveness, a crown of thorns, a cat-o'-nine-tails. Death. Yet he moved forward with purpose and passion.

He had only reached the outskirts of the city when word reached the townspeople that Jesus of Nazareth, the miracle worker, was entering Jerusalem. Excitement was at a fever pitch. First one, then many children began to run down the road followed by the men and then the women and finally the Pharisees and the Sadducees to meet Jesus. The religious leaders were angry and at the same time frightened, although they would not let it show on their faces. They did not run, but walked with an air of superiority and lack of concern, all the while wanting so badly to break out in a gallop toward the scene that lay ahead.

The crowds reached Jesus and his disciples and immediately

surrounded the clan like a raging flood escaping its banks would engulf and mold itself to the trunk of a great oak tree. The children, first to arrive, were pushed inward by the crowd that followed, against the sweat-soaked hair of the donkey and the colt. The discomfort they felt, though, paled in comparison to the joy they experienced at being within arm's reach of...

Who was this man they called Jesus? Why was everyone rushing to meet him? As the crowds swelled they began to sing to him. They shouted out praises to his name. They called him the Son of David. They blessed him as the one who came in the name of Yahweh.

Yet, in only four days, they would turn from a mob of worshipers to a mob thirsty for his blood. In only four days their exultations would turn to insults. They would turn on him and they would nail him to a cross.

Why?

The answer lies in one word: expectation.

The Jews had been oppressed for over 400 years. For generations their religious leaders had promised their flock a savior. Yet, in the most profound misunderstanding in all eternity, they preached the coming of a *military* leader rather than a *spiritual* leader. The people knew that a time would come when God would send a savior. The man they expected, however, was not understood to be a savior for the sins of all mankind. Rather, they expected the man to be a military leader sent to reign over an earthly Israelite kingdom and free the Jews from oppression. They envisioned this savior entering Jerusalem and establishing his earthly rule one day, setting the Israelites free from their earthly bondage.

Just as the crowds were shouting praises to his name, Jesus entered the borders of the city—as they expected.

He made his way toward the temple—as they expected.

He climbed the steps toward the temple gate—as they expected.

He then, in a matter of only minutes, entered the temple

area and, "drove out all who were buying and selling there." He overturned the tables of the moneychangers and the benches of those selling doves. "It is written," he said to them, "My house will be called a house of prayer, but you are making it a den of robbers" (Matthew 21:12–13).

They never, even in the most remote area of their collective mind, expected he would do that. With this one act, Jesus symbolically toppled the entire corrupt, self-serving religious structure of the Jewish people—his people—and they were not at all prepared. They could not have been prepared.

In the same way, I think many new believers are truly *unprepared* for what comes next in their newfound relationship with God.

Why?

For the same reason the Jews were unprepared. Expectation.

New believers many times have a skewed expectation of God because of well-intentioned but misguided Christians who have not given them a realistic picture of things to come. Ironically, we can show a new believer or non-Christian what to expect simply by explaining the meaning of both the Matthew 21 passage and the following verses:

> Do you not know that your body is *a temple of the Holy Spirit*, who is in you, whom you have received from God? You are not your own; you were bought at a price. Therefore honor God with your body (1 Corinthians 6:19–20).

The new believer, according to the above passage, becomes the "temple of the Holy Spirit"—the temple of God, where he resides. As God's present-day temple then, we can look to the passage in Matthew 21 to see how Jesus acted at the physical temple so we can get a crystal clear picture of how he will now act as he enters his new temple—the life of the believer.

Matthew 21:1–13 is the most profound example (and most

accurate account) in the Bible of what happens when someone becomes a Christian, allowing Jesus to be the ruler of his life. In this passage we see that what the Jews were completely unprepared for and what the new believer of today is unprepared to deal with, is the fact that when Jesus enters his temple he will act like—GOD!

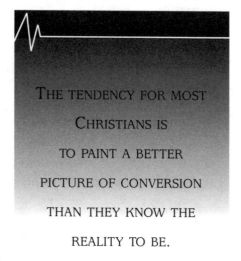

THE TENDENCY FOR MOST CHRISTIANS IS TO PAINT A BETTER PICTURE OF CONVERSION THAN THEY KNOW THE REALITY TO BE.

Jesus did exactly what he, being God in the flesh, would be expected to do. Go to *his* house (the temple) and drive out all who were trespassing on his turf! But the Jews were not expecting God in human form. They were expecting a man in military form. They weren't expecting a man who spoke with the authority of God. No, they were expecting a man with the autocratic persona of a great military leader. The penalty Jesus paid for not living up to their expectations was death—even death on a cross! (Philippians 2:8)

Those whom God places in our lives but who don't yet know him personally must be made aware of what happens when they give themselves to this Jesus—namely that Jesus comes into the life of a new believer, who is now the temple where the Spirit of God resides, and acts like himself! He does not ever adjust his persona to meet our expectations. He does not act in a manner different than his character demands. This is a vital piece to the evangelistic puzzle for several reasons.

First, some of us paint a rosy picture of life as a new believer, and in doing so we set up potential converts for extreme difficulty in the early stages of their relationships with God. Having realistic expectations is the key to the first days and weeks in the life of the new believer. The tendency for most Christians is to paint a better picture of conversion than they know the reality to be. We do this many times out of fear for the soul of the nonbeliever.

Another problem facing many believers who witness to adult unbelievers is that often the believer met Jesus at an early age. So they only know what it feels like to be forgiven for the list of sins they'd racked up in nine or ten years of life. But now they are talking to a coworker, for example, who has racked up thirty-five years of sin, the weight of which is simply unknowable to the believer who came to faith as a child! Equally as unknowable is the extent to which God must go to transform a thirty-five-year-old unbeliever.

Just as the Jews became angry at Jesus because he did not live up to their expectations, so do many new Christians get angry at God in the first days of their new relationship with him because they are *expecting* God to be someone he's not. They are expecting God to come in and be what they were told he would be by the well-intentioned Christian. So when God then comes into their lives, their temples, and cleans house as he did in the Jewish temple in Matthew 21, they get mad at God, turn away from the church and their new Christian friends and begin to wander aimlessly in the world from which they tried to escape. Many, as a result, are destined to spend years if not decades wandering in and out of churches, in and out of sin, extremely frustrated, finding very little if any progress in their relationship with God and feeling abandoned by their Christian friends, the church and God.

The second reason we must paint an accurate picture of God as he relates to a new believer is simple: precedent. We set a precedent for how the new believer will eventually witness as a mature believer. The new believer, if he survives the clash between expectation and reality in this new relationship with God, will, just as an abused child becomes an abusive parent, tell the same candy-coated story to his friends and coworkers. People inevitably teach what they are taught. They invariably lead in the same way they were led. This is a true conundrum of the human condition.

God Will Clean House

The most important thing we must tell the unbeliever or new believer is to expect Jesus to enter our temples, just as he entered the physical temple in Jerusalem, and clean house. In Jerusalem, Jesus didn't try to smooth things over with the religious authorities when it came to their sin of selling sacrificial animals for profit in the temple. He didn't suggest that they might try not to be so blatant about their sin or tell them that they could go on sinning as long as they did it quietly. No. He drove out all who were buying and selling in the temple (Matthew 21:12).

The first thing we must tell the seeking unbeliever as well as the new believer is that Jesus will come into that person's life and confront sin head on! As he confronted the sin of the religious leaders in the temple at Jerusalem, so will he confront the sins of the new believer. Essentially, when an unbeliever invites Jesus to establish his rule in his life, Jesus' first mission is to begin to clean the corruption from the "temple." Jesus' first words to the new believer are: "My house will be called a house of prayer, but you are making it a den of robbers" (Matthew 21:13). New believers can expect Jesus to move into their lives, his new temple, and begin to point out in detail the corruption that exists.

Mess ... What Mess?

My wife and I were eating dinner one evening. The plan was to eat, put the dishes in the dishwasher and then lie down on the couch together and watch a movie. Plans changed abruptly when we heard the doorbell ring.

"What? ... Who? ... Did you invite someone over tonight without telling me?" my wife whispered loudly as she grabbed my plate from underneath a fork full of food heading for my palate.

"Look at this house. It's a mess! There's stuff everywhere!" she exclaimed as I looked up from my now empty fork. I was about to blurt out something like, "The house isn't a mess, honey! It's probably just a late mail delivery or something ... " when I noticed that the house was "A MESS!!" I shouted.

Funny how neither one of us noticed the mess before the doorbell rang, I thought to myself. I began scooping up shoes and socks and magazines from the living room floor and throwing them into our bedroom as Julie went to answer the door. A couple of church members came by for a surprise visit and as Julie let them in I could hear her saying, "I'm so glad to see you two! Sorry for the messy house. We didn't think we'd have anybody over tonight." Fact is, we didn't even *see* the mess until someone came over that night. We had become so comfortable with the mess that we didn't consciously see it anymore.

In exactly the same fashion, unbelievers are completely unaware of the mess in their lives. They are blind to the piles of sin that are literally trashing their temples. Yet, when Jesus enters our lives we see for the first time through *his* eyes and suddenly we become painfully aware of the mess we've made. He opens our eyes to see the sin we simply could not see before he entered our lives. This can be a very difficult experience for some.

I, for example, had been piling up sin for twenty-four years before I invited Jesus into my life. So when he walked into my life, his new temple, and I saw what my life looked like through his eyes, it was an awful sight. Fortunately, I had been told what to expect. I had been properly prepared for the awakening. Todd Riddle told me to expect Jesus to come into my life and confront my sin. He said life would get harder before it got better. Granted, it got much harder than I expected, but then it got much better than I ever dreamed!

Never Trust the Weatherman

The other night I was watching the weather channel so I could decide what kind of clothes to pack for an upcoming youth retreat. The forecast called for partly cloudy skies and temperatures in the low to mid-

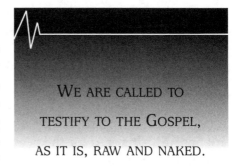

WE ARE CALLED TO TESTIFY TO THE GOSPEL, AS IT IS, RAW AND NAKED.

eighties. "Perfect!" I thought to myself. I proceeded to pack my favorite youth retreat uniform—shorts, T-shirts and my Teva sandals. A few days later I boarded my flight and sat back, opened a good book and settled in for a two-hour trip. Near the end of the flight, the stewardess came on the intercom announcing that we were in our final descent into Nashville.

"Welcome to Nashville International Airport. The time is approximately 2:35 p.m. The temperature in Nashville—a cool 62 degrees."

"Sixty-two degrees at 2:35 in the afternoon?" I inquired angrily of the man sitting next to me. He said nothing so I chose to express my anger at the person sitting across the aisle from me, "You can't trust the weatherman!"

I spent three days at the youth camp ill equipped for the ironic twist in the weather. My shorts, T-shirts and Teva sandals were no match for evenings in the mid-fifties and afternoons in the mid-sixties. I was so upset I promised myself I would never rely on the weatherman again.

If only I had known it was going to be cool, then at least I would have had cool-weather clothing and could have layered my clothes if it turned out to be cooler than expected. But the weather forecast was exactly the opposite of my expectation, which caused me to have a miserable weekend and distrust the weatherman.

New believers must be given an accurate forecast of things to come. If we paint a rosy forecast for new believers then all they know to prepare for is relative ease in their newfound relationships with God. Then, when all hell breaks loose in their lives, they become miserable and grow very quickly to distrust God and the Christians who gave them the wrong forecast. Yet if they are told that difficult times are ahead, then, even if they are not fully prepared for the degree of difficulty, they are still prepared for bad weather. The new believer who is prepared for bad weather will tend to weather the storm even if it is more severe than expected.

Curing This Evangelistic Cancer

Fear drives this evangelistic cancer of well-intentioned dishonesty in evangelism, and this fear comes from another misunderstanding in much of the Christian community. Many of us think that we are somehow responsible for the salvation of those to whom we witness. We think that we must talk a person into the kingdom rather than simply giving testimony of what God has done and will do. The candy-coated Gospel we preach comes from the mouths of us who are afraid that if we don't paint a pleasing enough picture, then the nonbeliever will not respond to God. Yet we are not the ones who save people. God saves people. We are not the ones who are responsible for how someone responds to the Gospel. God is.

Paul explains this truth eloquently in Ephesians. In writing his letter to the church at Ephesus, Paul reminds the believers of their condition prior to the death and resurrection of Jesus and exactly how they came to be part of the family of God:

> As for you, you were dead in your transgressions and sins ... but because of his great love for us, *God*, who is rich in mercy, *made us alive with Christ* even when we were dead in transgressions—*it is by grace you have been saved* (Ephesians 2:1, 4–5).

Salvation is from God by grace. This passage reminded the believers of the early church and reminds the believer today that God is the one who "makes us alive together with Christ." He is ultimately and solely responsible for the salvation of every person and nothing we do or say will keep him from accomplishing his will! This gives us radical freedom when it comes to sharing our faith. We do not need to candy-coat the Gospel, make it sound more acceptable or persuade anyone to accept the free gift of salvation that comes from God.

We are called to testify to the Gospel, as it is, raw and naked. We must walk into every evangelistic opportunity with a steadfast belief in what Paul described in his first letter to the church in Corinth:

> *For Christ did not send me to baptize, but to preach the gospel—not with words of human wisdom, lest the cross of Christ be emptied of its power. For the message of the cross is foolishness to those who are perishing, but to us who are being saved it is the power of God.* For it is written: "I will destroy the wisdom of the wise; the intelligence of the intelligent I will frustrate." Where is the wise man? Where is the scholar? Where is the philosopher of this age? Has not God made foolish the wisdom of the world? For since in the wisdom of God the world through its wisdom did not know him, *God was pleased through the foolishness of what was preached to save those who believe.* Jews demand miraculous signs and Greeks look for wisdom, but we preach Christ crucified: a stumbling block to Jews and foolishness to Gentiles, but to those whom God has called, both Jews and Greeks, Christ the power of God and the wisdom of God. For the foolishness of God is wiser than man's wisdom, and the weakness of God is stronger than man's strength. Brothers, think of what you were when you were called. Not many of you were wise by human standards; not many were influential; not many were of

noble birth. But God chose the foolish things of the world to shame the wise; God chose the weak things of the world to shame the strong. He chose the lowly things of this world and the despised things—and the things that are not—to nullify the things that are, so that no one may boast before him. It is because of him that you are in Christ Jesus, who has become for us wisdom from God—that is, our righteousness, holiness and redemption. Therefore, as it is written: "Let him who boasts boast in the Lord" (1 Corinthians 1:17–31).

The true Gospel of Jesus Christ is foolishness to an unbelieving world. The Gospel cannot be defended with worldly logic. God proposed to make the claims of the Gospel impossible to be validated by worldly wisdom (1 Corinthians 1:21). Rather it is only by sharing the Gospel in its raw, unimpressive, foolish state that it can and will be used by God to make all those who would respond to its truth alive together with Christ (Ephesians 2:5).

We must add nothing to this message of truth "lest the cross of Christ be emptied of its power" (1 Corinthians 1:17). We must not attempt to convince others of its merit, but only to tell of Jesus, and him crucified on the cross for the sins of the world. We also must not attempt to hide the truth of the hardships that await the new believer on the other side of salvation. The message of the cross has been created and explained by the God of infinite wisdom and cannot in any way be made better or more palatable than it is. It simply is what it is. No more and no less.

17

Getting Something vs.
Becoming Someone

God tells us that "all have sinned and fall short of God's plan" (Romans 3:23).

That night in front of a thousand or more young people, the silence was so thick, so substantive that it seemed to beg for its own survival. What was only two seconds in actual time became an eternity. The inevitable words seemed unwelcome, and at the same time anticipation grew, for many in the room knew what I knew of those unspoken words to come—they brought with them eternal life.

"God goes on to say that the payment for sin is death, but the free gift of God is eternal life through Jesus."

In spite of the blinding lights I could just make out silhouettes of people in the front rows nodding their heads in agreement with every word. They knew what was coming. They sensed what I sensed. They felt what I felt.

"God showed his love for you and me in a special way. How

does God show love? He gave his Son for each one of us; not when we have our act together but while we are yet sinners, he sent Jesus to die for you and me personally. Why? So that Jesus would pay the penalty for our sins."

Two or three in the audience who became animated by their heartfelt expectation clapped once or twice seemingly unaware that it was their hands making the noise. They stopped themselves in submission to the moment.

"Therefore, if we would only proclaim that Jesus is the Lord of our lives, if we would only believe in our hearts that God truly raised him from the dead, then we would be saved!"

I continued at a quickening pace.

"You may be sitting there right now thinking to yourself, 'If this God he speaks of really exists and he really wants to know me personally then I want to know him, too! If he really wants to forgive me for all the bad stuff I've done, then I'm in!' Well, he does! You can do business with God right where you are sitting tonight. You have the opportunity to meet God personally tonight and start a relationship with him that lasts forever! From the moment you meet him tonight, nothing you ever do, nothing anyone ever says from that moment on will ever, ever separate you from God."

Perhaps many believers in the audience were remembering the moment they started their own relationship with God. Maybe some were watching and listening to everything through the eyes and ears of the friend who sat next to them, hearing each word and imagining what must be going through the mind of their un-churched friend, hoping that each word was piercing the heart of that friend for whom they had prayed so long.

"Right now I'm going to lead all of you in a prayer to God. Now understand that if you repeat every word perfectly in this prayer it means absolutely nothing unless you believe what you are about to speak in your heart. What you are about to say is not some chant or incantation that, if said in proper order, earns you your membership card in heaven. No. This moment rests solely on the condition of your heart. If you are sitting there tonight and know that you have never met God personally but you want to meet him tonight, just tell God. You can speak these words aloud or in total silence from your heart. God will hear you either way. Just tell him tonight, 'I don't know you, God, but I want to know you personally. I realize that you sent your Son, Jesus, to die on the cross for me. So I turn from my old life right now and turn to you and ask you to forgive me for all my sins and start a relationship with me that lasts forever. God, thank you for saving me.'"

Whispers of those echoing the words came from everywhere in the audience.

"If you just spoke those words to God and meant them in your heart I want you to just raise your hand in the air right now."

Dozens and dozens of hands rose above the sea of bowed heads.

"Those of you who spoke those words to God now have an eternal address in heaven! You are breathing eternally right at this moment. You have been forgiven of all your sins! You have a clean slate! You've been born into the family of God tonight. You are an heir to his kingdom! Tonight, when you lay your head on your pillow you can know that for all eternity nothing you ever do, nothing anyone ever says can ever separate you from your relationship with God."

That night over fifty young people met our prayer team after the service to acknowledge that they had done business with God that night. They responded to the plea that was made from the stage to surrender their lives to Jesus. I was taken aback by the response to the message that night.

But ...

What was the message to which they responded?

To what or whom were they surrendering?

What had they done that night?

What, if anything had God done that night?

This chapter may create some angst in your heart if you choose not to read it in its entirety. If it is not read with great intent, you will most certainly miss the point and, possibly, the point of the entire book. The stated purpose of this book is to first teach you *why* we are called by God to share the Good News, and only then proceed to tell you *how* to share the Good News through God-empowered relationships. This stated purpose begs the question: What is the Good News?

How can I possibly ask this question? After all, the Good News is so simple! How could a chapter possibly be devoted to the explanation of the Gospel? Why would I suppose that the majority of Christians today would need an explanation of the Gospel?

My supposition comes from the fact that in my Christian walk I have only recently become aware of a profound flaw in my understanding of the Good News. This flaw is not one of my own creation, rather it is *the* prevalent view in mainstream American Christianity today. This flaw is what is offered to people every day from pulpits across America, in Sunday school classes, at dinner tables and office break rooms. I preached this very flaw that night in front of those many young people looking for the Good News. We as Christians are offering okay news as Gospel rather than the Good News the Bible promises.

What can I possibly be talking about?

The answer lies in the needed shift in our thinking from what we *get from God*, to who we actually *become in God*. The Gospel that was offered to me and the Gospel I have offered on behalf of God to thousands of people is an offer to get something from God, rather than the more profound offer to become someone in God!

When someone is offered the okay Gospel of getting an address in heaven and having God forgive them of their sin so they don't have to spend eternity in hell, it is not a counterfeit

Gospel. But it most certainly is not a complete Gospel. The most profound truth in all eternity is not that we can be saved from hell or even that we can live for eternity in heaven—but that we literally become children of God!

Just Another Day in America

In the fall of 2002 authorities captured two individuals responsible for sniper murders in and around Virginia. Ten people were killed by sniper fire in less than three weeks. The entire region was terrified and many chose to hide in their homes trying to wait out the drama in relative safety.

If you remember the news reports at the time, you probably felt as I did. Although living in Texas, far away from the shootings, I hurt for those people living in fear. I was angry with the person or persons responsible and had an extremely difficult time praying for them. I wanted them caught and imprisoned for life—or worse.

John Muhammad and Lee Boyd Malvo were caught and faced the possibility of the death penalty. Thousands of citizens were permanently scarred by the actions of these men and they deserved the harshest of punishment.

Now ...

What if I told you that the President of the United States had sent a memo to Lee Boyd Malvo, the seventeen-year-old gunman, saying that he would grant Malvo a presidential pardon for the murders he committed? What if I told you that Malvo gladly accepted the pardon and walked out of prison a free man? You

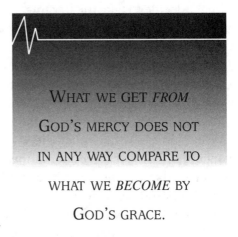

WHAT WE GET *FROM* GOD'S MERCY DOES NOT IN ANY WAY COMPARE TO WHAT WE *BECOME* BY GOD'S GRACE.

know, of course, that Bush did not grant Malvo a pardon for his crimes. However, what effect do you think a pardon would have on a young man with such hatred and disdain for his fellow man, his family, and his country? Do you think Malvo would change his ways? Would Malvo become a model citizen? Would he be so appreciative of his opportunity to dodge death or life in prison that he would begin touring the country warning young people of the destructive nature of hate? Not likely. We would like to think that any criminal who is granted a pardon or early parole would be so thankful that he would spend the rest of his life giving back to the society that showed him mercy. Often, however, this is not the case. Mercy has never been enough to change the average man.

More likely, Malvo would resume his deadly mission until caught again. More likely, if given the chance, he would renew and even step up the pace of his killing spree. Mercy would not have been the transforming agent. Mercy would only have allowed the same man with the same stone heart to commit the same cold acts of murder.

We as a society would also be outraged at the news of a presidential pardon! We would cry foul from the rooftops and some might decide to take the law into their own hands and enact the punishment on Malvo that government failed to carry out.

Let us now take the scenario a step further. Instead of simply granting Malvo a reprieve from his crimes, let's say the president also offered to legally adopt the young man into his family. Malvo would then be the son of the President of the United States. He would live and play and enjoy the comforts of the White House. When asked, he would go into the details of his encounter with the president, now his adopted father, and the changes that this newfound love relationship had made in his life. He would describe his crimes and account for the mercy he received, but he would also go into great detail about who he had *become* by the grace of a stranger.

Grace is the changing force in our lives as Christians and

our understanding of this unmerited grace compels us to share with others the grace available to them also. Our reprieve from hell is not transforming. Rather, it is the adoption into the family of the King that changes our lives forever. In other words, the Good News is not only that we are granted a merciful reprieve from our sentence to eternity in hell, but that we also become children of God! What we *get from* God's mercy does not in any way compare to what we *become* by God's grace. God's mercy grants us a reprieve from hell. God's grace enables us to become children of God. Grace changes people from hopeless to hope-filled, restless to restful, bitter to boastful in him who saves. Grace is at the center of our redemption.

Getting out of hell or even getting into heaven pales in comparison to the richness of the grace bestowed on us while it is still today.

Peter and the disciples came face to face with the abundant grace bestowed on them in life when they were with Jesus after his discussion with the man who asked, "what must I do to inherit eternal life?" Jesus tells him to sell everything he has and give it all to the poor and he will then have a place in heaven. The story records that the man "went sadly away because he had many possessions." The story continues in Mark 10:

> Jesus looked around and said to his disciples, "How hard it is for rich people to get into the Kingdom of God!" This amazed them. But Jesus said again, "Dear children, it is very hard to get into the Kingdom of God. It is easier for a camel to go through the eye of a needle than for a rich person to enter the Kingdom of God!" The disciples were astounded. "Then who in the world can be saved?" they asked. Jesus looked at them intently and said, "Humanly speaking, it is impossible. But not with God. Everything is possible with God." Then Peter began to mention all that he and the other disciples had left behind. "We've given up everything to follow you,"

he said. And Jesus replied, "I assure you that everyone who has given up house or brothers or sisters or mother or father or children or property, for my sake and for the Good News, will receive now in return, a hundred times over, houses, brothers, sisters, mothers, children, and property—with persecutions. And in the world to come they will have eternal life. But many who seem to be important now will be the least important then, and those who are considered least here will be the greatest then" (Mark 10:23–31 NLT).

Jesus promises that the things they turned from to follow him and proclaim the Gospel, they will *now* receive a hundred times more. Note the promises: houses and property are in the mix but the list is redundant in his promises to them for—*relationships*! He then mentions that they will, of course, also get eternal life. The interesting part of this passage is the inclusion of the promise of persecution in this present day as well. This was not a warning. In fact, it is the final blessing in the list of many blessings to expect!

How can I come to the conclusion that the persecution was part of the promised hundred-fold blessing? Paul proves it in his letter to Rome and in his letter to the church in Philippi. First to the Philippians:

> As a result, I can really know Christ and experience the mighty power that raised him from the dead. *I can learn what it means to suffer with him, sharing in his death*, so that, somehow, I can experience the resurrection from the dead (Philippians 3:10–11 NLT).

Then to the Romans:

> And since we are his children, we will share his treasures—for everything God gives to his Son, Christ,

is ours, too. But if we are to share his glory, *we must also share his suffering* (Romans 8:17 NLT).

Paul came to understand and even pursue the fruit of sharing in the sufferings of Christ, and at the same time he learned the futility of any effort to avoid suffering and loss and persecution.

Where is the grace of this relationship with Jesus expressed at its highest level? Is it in the possessions? No. Is it in the eternal life to come? No. Is it in the promise of persecution? No. *The emphasis is on relationships!*

Whatever the promise, the emphasis was not ultimately on the *what* but the *when*. The blessings were to be for today. The grace given to us from God is to be not only experienced today but also shared today. Our adoption papers have been signed. We are invited to take our seat at the family table of the King of all kings. We are children. We are in relationship with him. We are the body of Christ. Yes, we get out of hell and get into heaven but we are children of God—today! Our identity is forever altered. We are no longer the sinner saved by grace. Rather, we are children of God, heirs to the kingdom of God, a royal priesthood, a holy nation. We are the saints of God who at times fall into sin. We are made righteous in his sight because of the sacrifice he made on our behalf through his only Son, Jesus.

The grace is not fully expressed in the getting of something. The grace is expressed and realized in *becoming someone!*

That is the Good News! That is the Gospel! That is the promise we are to share to all nations. That is the promise to Malvo and Hitler and Bundy and your best friend and my boss and my neighbor and even me. We can all *become* children of God!

My point then is this: We must offer to those around us the true message of the cross. People are not changed or altered fundamentally by our promise of a "Get Out of Hell Free" card.

They do not alter their lifestyles in daily submission to the God from whom they received their "fire insurance policy."

They must be told of the powerful opportunity God has given them to die to their old ways. We must offer the promise to everyone that we can die to all that has gone before. They can truly bury forever the person they have become in their sinful world as a result of their sinful choices. We must explain with clarity and conviction that they can be reborn as new creations, children born from the very womb of God. They must know that we are now bound by a blood tie so substantial that our earthly family ties are but shadows in comparison.

To preach anything less is to trivialize the cross. We must share the full, dynamic, unbelievable, enigmatic, impossible, glorious, frightening, awesome Gospel that God offers to everyone.

18

The Power of Simply
Being Present

In the church today ministry has become about the crowd, the cause, and the people. When I say people I'm talking about the group. I can honestly say that I'm passionate about reaching a generation for Christ. I can honestly say that I am passionate about changing the world. I can say with conviction that I am passionate about changing the spiritual tide of this nation. I am very passionate about God and the Bible and theology.

In the church today we have almost completely lost sight of the individual. We have passion for our generation, the event, the cause, the nation, but we have not fostered a passion for the individual in the church today. Ministry today is defined in many ways by its ability to bring in a crowd. Ministers' careers are weighed and given worth based on their ability to draw the crowd.

As I've mentioned before, I spent five years teaching at a

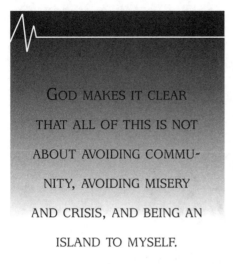

GOD MAKES IT CLEAR THAT ALL OF THIS IS NOT ABOUT AVOIDING COMMUNITY, AVOIDING MISERY AND CRISIS, AND BEING AN ISLAND TO MYSELF.

weekly event in San Antonio, Texas called San Antonio Metro. Hundreds of young adults attended every week for five years. I can honestly say that I was overwhelmingly passionate about the crowd. I taught the masses every week. I stood in front of the people to share the Bible. The difficulty came when I had to get off stage, go to the back of the room after the event, and dive into the lives of individual people. Everything in my flesh fights this reality. Everything in me in many ways despises this paradox. Yet at the same time, everything of God in me compels me to embrace this truth.

Having passion for the crowd is easy. Having passion for the event is a piece of cake. Having passion for the programs in our churches is nothing to brag about. Having a passion for the individual though, is in every way impossible without a deep understanding of the character of God and a sense of constant intimacy in your relationship with him.

The way I look at it, I have enough problems of my own. So if I add your problems to my problems, then I definitely have too many problems. Yet God makes it clear that all of this is not about avoiding community, avoiding misery and crisis, and being an island to myself. Rather it is about taking all of my problems (that I can barely deal with now) and adding you and your problems to my life!

You want passion? Dive in. Get down deep into the misery of another individual.

I've Never Liked Hospitals

I was sharing with a close friend that I have tremendous difficulty going to hospitals for *any* reason. I explained to him how confused I was at times by the fact that God chose me to be a pastor. In fact, I dislike going to hospitals so much that I require my ministry responsibilities not include visiting people in the hospital.

He told me about a friend going through chemotherapy for cancer whom he visited regularly. But, he said,

> "There's a huge difference between calling him on the phone at the hospital, dropping by every other day or so to visit with him or sending a note of encouragement ... and choosing to meet him on the day of his release from the hospital at his home and deciding to stay with him through the aftermath of his chemotherapy, wiping his chapped and cracking lips after he wraps his hands around the toilet for the fifth time in an hour to throw up, staying up with him as he finds it impossible to sleep because of the pain, wrapping him with a warm blanket and holding him as he shivers in a cold sweat."

Calling and saying "I'm praying for you" is very different from asking if you can spend the next few days with your friend climbing down into the pit of his misery.

We have lost sight of God's perspective of things. We have lost sight of the importance of the individual, and instead have given great importance to the crowd and to the crowd-makers.

What Did Jesus Do?

Jesus walked through crowds and spoke to crowds for what purpose? He walked through and talked to the crowd to find the individual. He left the crowds to minister to the individual. The crowd wasn't bad or wrong for being there. Neither was Jesus being insensitive for focusing on just one. He sought out those individuals who needed him. He wanted to change lives, yes. But he changed lives one life at a time. The examples are almost too numerous to reference: Zacchaeus, the woman at the well, Matthew, the Gerasene Demoniac.

The church today talks about the individual sporadically but focuses its staff, its budgets and its praises on the crowd. Yet God always gives importance to the one.

In our earlier look at Luke 15, I mentioned that I would have fired the shepherd who left ninety-nine sheep in his care and went after the one that got lost in the wilderness. The potential is great that the shepherd would set out to find the lost sheep, which might already be dead, only to get lost himself and die. Then the ninety-nine sheep would start scattering and they would all die—and now everyone is dead!

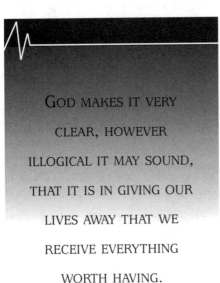

GOD MAKES IT VERY CLEAR, HOWEVER ILLOGICAL IT MAY SOUND, THAT IT IS IN GIVING OUR LIVES AWAY THAT WE RECEIVE EVERYTHING WORTH HAVING.

If I'm the shepherd, I'd stay with the ninety-nine sheep and begin to do some sort of sheep call to try to coax the lost sheep back into the fold. I'd wait for a minute or two and then, if he didn't come back, I'd move on without him.

What about the woman with the ten coins? Here you have an obviously obsessive-compulsive young lady who has ten coins and loses one of them. I don't care how big the coins are, she still has nine after losing only one. But she frantically moves furniture and sweeps the entire house to find this one coin. I have lost many coins before. Several dollars' worth of coins were found between the cushions of our couch in a recent move. There was no prior thought to finding them. I didn't turn over the furniture and search the entire house for those coins. Yet this woman does just that. Then, upon finding the coin, she opens her front door and shouts to her neighbors.

"I've found my coin! Let's spend the other nine coins having a party in recognition of my success at finding this one coin!"

Jesus would say, "Way to go, good shepherd! Way to go, woman! You have done a good thing. This is exactly what the kingdom of God is about!"

In fact, everything in the Bible from Genesis to Revelation is centered on revealing the importance of the individual to God. The act of creating a man, Adam, rather then men; the revelation of God's character through the mouths of his prophets in the Old Testament; the act of becoming man in the person of Jesus to live a sinless life and eventually die for each one of us; writing these truths through the apostles, Paul, and the other writers of the New Testament, revealing even more of who he is and how he desires to relate with us—everything screams of the importance of the one.

Yet the focus on the event seems to cast a far different shadow upon the church. We begin to see the event as the prize. Culture looks inside the church and sees the value we place on the crowd. The crowd has gained so much value in the minds and hearts of the leaders of the church today that we conclude that as long as the crowd gathers, losing one or a few is just part of the process. We have resigned ourselves, even defended what most would call an established fact—that we're going to lose one or two sheep in the process of building the crowd. So be it. We still have a crowd.

So we exalt the crowd. We disregard those who fall through the cracks as collateral damage in the fight to win the world to

Jesus. Yet Jesus tells us that all of creation was fashioned, our very salvation was offered, through the sacrifice of the one for the individual and we are to take that message to the masses one person at a time.

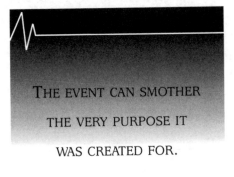

THE EVENT CAN SMOTHER

THE VERY PURPOSE IT

WAS CREATED FOR.

God's Word is in stark contrast to the institution we call the church today. The things we spend our money and time on— building structures and maintaining them, assembling massive staffs to create and run programs for the express purpose of feeding the ninety-nine sheep already in the fold—would not be where Jesus would spend most of his time or his money.

Event-driven Madness

With sadness in my heart, I confess I have not left the ninety-nine to go after the one lost sheep. I'm concerned that at my very essence I am focused on the ninety-nine—the cause, the crowd, changing the world—and have put relatively little effort in diving into the misery of those individuals whose eyes tell the tale of sorrow and whose hearts need mending. By giving much of my time to creating and maintaining events, I have in many ways fostered this skewed perspective and in effect, proclaimed that the loss of a few sheep is just part of the process of fighting the good fight—and that simply cannot be.

I remember a time at San Antonio Metro, the weekly event where I preached for five years, when fifty or sixty people responded to my invitation to start a relationship with Jesus. I was thrilled at the very core of my being. As the band began to play the closing song, I invited those who had made a decision to meet me in the foyer during the song so that I and the other counselors could talk with them, pray with them, and answer their questions. I walked quickly to the back of the worship center to meet the people who responded.

Within several minutes over fifty people surrounded me. I could count only eight or nine behind the crowd with counselor tags on who were trained to minister to these new Christians. They were trained to sit down with these people individually, answer their questions, welcome them into the family of God and try to connect them to a local church.

I peered over the heads of these new believers and caught the eye of a young lady who was on the Metro leadership team. She was standing behind the resources table where we offered tapes of the messages each week. She and another member of our leadership team stood there behind the table as though nothing paramount was happening right in front of their eyes. I formed words silently with my lips while motioning for them to come over to help me.

"Get over here! We need you!"

She looked back and shrugged her shoulders.

"There's no one else to cover the resource table," she said.

I was shocked and angry at the situation that was unfolding.

Fifty or more new members of an eternal family to which I belonged were born only moments ago and the nurses in charge of cleaning and wrapping a warm blanket around the newborns were standing by the hospital phone in case a call came in.

I made my way through the crowd of new believers, approached the resource table and said with an air of frustration, "Put a sign on the table that says 'everything is free,' and come spend some quality time with our new brothers and sisters."

I then walked back into the worship center as the last song played, grabbed the microphone and made it known that a wonderful thing was happening tonight and we were in need of thirty to forty more people to sit and talk and pray with these new believers. I also told them that there would be no one at the door to say good night to them and the resource table was not manned. They could simply take the tapes they needed and pay at a later date.

Many people volunteered to help and each new Christian had an opportunity to talk with an older believer about living a life with Jesus and the importance of finding a church home. I also knew that ultimately God had the situation under control, but my eyes were opened that night, unlike any time before or since, to the fact that the event can smother the very purpose it was created for.

I later spoke with our leadership team and made a very clear statement:

"There is nothing more important in this ministry than the new believer. There will never be another time when the resource table is perceived to be more important than a new believer's first minutes of eternal life. The greeters at the door are greeters only until there is a need for them to minister to a new believer. The worship team can continue playing only as long as they are not needed to minister to a new believer. Nothing is of greater value or merits our attention and focus more than the new believer."

I take responsibility for the lack of education of our leaders that led to the potential crisis of that night. I trained them, saying that every job was important and that it was important that we all be in our places. I failed to teach them, however, why we were truly there, and that everything was optional in light of an individual's need for guidance in their newfound relationship with God. I also became keenly and painfully aware of the ease by which the church today can exalt the event and devalue the individual.

Who's Missing?

My greatest concern in the church today is that we have so devalued the individual that we don't even know if he or she is missing. Even if we notice he or she is missing, the goal is not to go out and find him or her. The goal is to bring him or her back—to the group!

In Sunday school class in a Southern Baptist church I attended, one man was assigned to call the people who didn't show up for Sunday school and invite them back—to the group. I heard him at the church one day calling people. He called around noon on a weekday so he was leaving a lot of messages. He would say something like this: "Hey, John, *we* noticed you were missing in Sunday school last Sunday and *we* just wanted to tell you that *we* hope to see you back with the *group* next week."

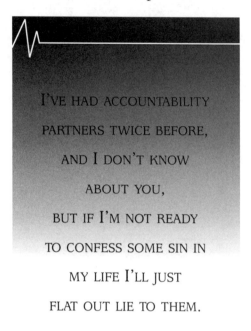

I'VE HAD ACCOUNTABILITY PARTNERS TWICE BEFORE, AND I DON'T KNOW ABOUT YOU, BUT IF I'M NOT READY TO CONFESS SOME SIN IN MY LIFE I'LL JUST FLAT OUT LIE TO THEM.

Basically, we were telling those people that we're in the group and you're not. We would like to have you back in the group, because we're all in—the group.

When I first began to attend a church regularly after my salvation experience, I received one of those very messages.

"*We* noticed you were missing this Sunday. *We* sure were glad to see you last Sunday and *we* would love to see you next Sunday."

The person left no phone number to call if I had questions. He didn't even leave a name. Do you know why? Because *he* wasn't calling. "*We*" were calling!

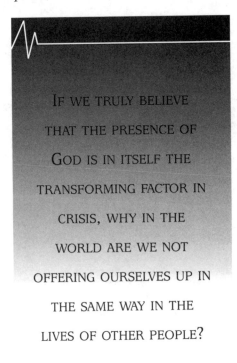

IF WE TRULY BELIEVE THAT THE PRESENCE OF GOD IS IN ITSELF THE TRANSFORMING FACTOR IN CRISIS, WHY IN THE WORLD ARE WE NOT OFFERING OURSELVES UP IN THE SAME WAY IN THE LIVES OF OTHER PEOPLE?

"We, the group, we're all calling! We are all calling you—to come back to the group."

I had a real problem with the whole situation. The voice mail ended with, "We hope you come back to see *us*. We'd sure like to see you. In fact, we are having a potluck ... next Wednesday night and we'd like to see you there."

Is it wrong to make those calls as a church to reach out to those who are absent? Absolutely not! If you are the person who made a call like that just last week, I am not trying to negate or trivialize what you did. But know this for certain. People don't need *us* to call. They need *you* to call. If you have to leave a message, leave one they want to hear.

"Hi, this is Todd Phillips from your Sunday school class at ABC Church. *I* don't know if you remember me but *I* remember *you*. *I* haven't seen *you* in two weeks so *I* asked the class director for *your* number so *I* could call *you*. I want to leave *my* phone number so *you* can call *me* and *I* thought we might be able to meet for lunch next week. *I'll* call *you* back if I haven't heard from *you* in the next few days."

We must go to the individual. We must leave the flock and go to the individual out in the wilderness. We must not simply yell from the flock an invitation to come back to the flock. We must leave the flock in search of the one.

The shepherd was right. The woman who lost her coin was right on the money—so to speak.

Do you know when they are missing?

Do you leave the crowd to find them?

Does Anybody Know When You're Missing?

This is a subject I left until now for a reason. I think many of us are entrenched in this group mentality because it is all we know. We don't expect anyone to leave the flock to find us if we're missing. I'm not talking, by the way, about you not being physically present. I'm talking about someone in your life who knows when you're there physically but not there mentally or spiritually.

Do you have anyone who dives into your misery, searches for you in your world, where you are, and spends time there with you? Does anyone know you well enough to know when you are missing? Before we go any further down this trail I want to make it clear that I am not referring to your accountability partner. I'm so tired of people asking me who my accountability partner is. It's cool right now in the church to have someone in your life who is your official accountability partner, but I've had accountability partners twice before, and I don't know about you, but if I'm not ready to confess some sin in my life I'll just flat out lie to them.

"Todd, are you entertaining any sexually impure thoughts?"

"Absolutely not. My thoughts have been pure as the driven snow since you asked me the same question last week." If I'm not ready to deal with something in my life, then my official accountability partner isn't going to force me to deal with it.

So I'm not asking if you have an accountability partner. I'm asking if you have someone who dives into your life for the sole purpose of being present. There is a huge difference. Who constantly lets his presence be known? Can you write that one name down? Not your Bible study partner or your Sunday school director or even your best friend from high school that you stay in touch with at least once a month. It could be any one of these people, but is that person in your world?

This person loves you unconditionally. He or she is there no matter what and seems to show up at the times of greatest crisis just to be present. This is the person who will leave the flock every time to find you.

Your spouse, if you have one, should be one of these people in your life. But, I would argue, there must be another, of the same sex, not in your circle of daily influence, not a coworker. It should be someone older *and* wiser. Not older and dumber, older and wiser! You need to find that person who has been through what you've been through and what you have yet to go through and who has made good choices. You don't want a guy who says, "Yeah, been there. Pretty tough, huh?"

A Parable

A teacher came to his student and asked, "Do you love me?"
The student replied, "Yes, teacher, I love you."
The teacher asked again, "Do you love me?"
Again the student replied, "Yes, of course I do."
The teacher then asked, "Do you know what causes me grief? Do you know the source of the misery deep in my heart?"
"No," replied the student.
"Then," said the teacher, "how can you possibly love me?"
People are desperate for even one person to just be present, not to fix things, not to call them on the carpet, but to simply be present. For in that presence comes understanding.

Would you not agree that in the midst of crisis, the knowledge that Jesus is present in your time of need is transforming? Knowing that God has promised to never leave you or forsake you is sufficient. Yet, we spend all our time as God's children trying to fix other people. As ministers, we want to hear the problem, box it into a category of sin, reference a passage of Scripture, pray for them and be done.

If we truly believe that the presence of God is in itself the transforming factor in crisis, why in the world are we not offering ourselves up in the same way in the lives of other people? Am I saying not to hold your friends or yourself accountable? Of course not. But we all need that one person who derives his own godly passion from sharing in our sufferings. We must always remember that we are also empowered to be that individual for someone else!

What is the Gospel? What is the Good News? It is God's grace expressed in the person of Jesus Christ and through his life, death, burial, and resurrection so that whosoever believes in him will not be eternally separated from God, but will possess an eternal, intimate, family relationship with God himself! The Good News is for the "whosoever"! The Good News is not that "God loved the world ..." but that *because* God loved the world he gave every *individual* human being the opportunity to begin an everlasting relationship with him! All of history, all of creation exists to proclaim this specific, individualized love that God has for every ONE of us.

19

Apologetics Problem: No One Is Ever Argued into the Kingdom

Let's take some time to look at the subject of apologetics to clarify its meaning and purpose and see how it relates to evangelism. Apologetics is a powerful tool—a powerful tool not primarily for witnessing to the nonbeliever, however, but for increasing the faith of the believer. This may be the most controversial chapter of the book. The long-standing view of most mainline denominations is that apologetics is a powerful and effective tool for use by any and all believers to witness to any and all nonbelievers. This is just not the case. The Merriam-Webster Dictionary Web site (at www.m-w.com) cites two definitions for apologetics:

> 1. Systematic argumentative discourse in defense (as of a doctrine).
> 2. A branch of theology devoted to the defense of the divine origin and authority of Christianity.

There is a vast difference between the concept of using apologetics as an evangelistic tool and using apologetics as a tool for defending or proving the doctrines of Christianity against other ideologies and philosophies in culture. In fact, apologetics throughout history has been a methodology by which a believer can use the premise of scholarly reason to defend Christian doctrine as a plausible religion, philosophy, or ideology. The ultimate motive of apologetics then is not to convert a person to Christianity, but to rhetorically defend the merits of Christian doctrine over other doctrines. The defense itself is the goal of apologetics, not the response of the one to whom the defense is directed.

You might say that the act of witnessing has the same goal—of simply speaking the Good News with no concern for the response. You would be right. Most understand apologetics as a tool that inherently demands a response. This view forces apologetics into offensive tactics that attempt to argue the hearer into converting to Christianity rather than remaining a defensive proclamation of the merits of the Christian faith.

Can God use an apologetic argument to bring someone to himself? Absolutely! God used a donkey to speak to Balaam in Numbers 22, but this is not the biblical norm. Donkeys are not God's primary form of communication with man. God makes this very clear:

> In the past God spoke to our forefathers through the prophets at many times and in various ways, but in these last days he has spoken to us by his Son, whom he appointed heir of all things, and through whom he made the universe (Hebrews 1:1–2).

Here God shows his preferred forms of communication—prophets and the person of Jesus.

So what was the primary evangelistic tool in the early days

of the church? In what form or by what manner was the Gospel shared? These questions beg an argument from some who would suggest that the examples of witnessing in the Bible couldn't be considered mandates for evangelistic methodology today. Those same people would argue that the fact that stories were the main methodology of early church evangelism does not give us the de facto principle by which we should share the Gospel today. After all, they would say, times were different. The culture was more religious. Today we must first use apologetics to defend and validate the origins of the Bible and then we can share our faith experience. Some might even say that simply sharing our faith experience does nothing to defend the faith and that a defense founded on reason is a must, especially in today's advanced society.

I wholeheartedly disagree.

I believed in this line of reasoning as a young believer. I believed then that I had to win people to Jesus through reason and rhetoric. I have many examples from my early witnessing days that give credence to my supposition. My favorite example lies in a conversation I had with an old friend.

Soon after I began my relationship with Jesus I received a call from an old friend, John Ogleton. He was a tall, strapping, handsome, African-American man who had a striking resemblance to Malcolm X. John and I met in 1987, well before my conversion to Christianity. He was quite wrapped up in the events surrounding my salvation experience in Denver only months before and was calling to ask some questions about the "whole religion thing I had going."

He wanted to get together over coffee and talk and suggested we meet in a few days. I agreed, hung up the phone, and began to panic. I raised my eyes toward the ceiling and began an impromptu discussion with God.

"My first opportunity to share my faith with a nonbeliever and, of course, it would have to be my highly intelligent and quick-witted friend John. How am I supposed to share my faith with a man whose picture is right next to the word 'brilliant' in the dictionary?"

Not waiting for a response from God (which I should have), I called a pastor friend of mine at Hyde Park Baptist Church and asked if I could borrow all the books and periodicals he had on defending the faith (apologetics). He obliged and I went immediately to his office to pick them up. I reasoned that I would have to prove to John that the Bible was truly the Word of God, that it was not merely a religious book like the Koran or the Egyptian Book of The Dead, but the literal textual representation of the eternal wisdom from the mouth of the one and only God of the Universe.

I studied furiously as our meeting approached. I was feverishly gathering together proofs of the Bible's authority and validating not only the work itself, but also every statement written in it that claimed that Jesus was the Savior of the world.

As the morning of our meeting came I felt completely unprepared to talk with John. After all, I believed, if I messed anything up, if I said something wrong or spoke an untruth, well, John might be damned to hell!

I called him just hours before our meeting and apologized for the late notice, told him something came up and rescheduled for the same day and time the following week. John obliged and I was finally able to breathe, feeling that, at least for the moment, I was free from the awesome responsibility of John's salvation.

I knew in my young Christian heart that God was completely in control of the conversation I would have with John. Not only was God in control of our conversation, but God was also in control of John's eternal reality. I knew that God was the one who would make John "alive together with Christ," but I was still mapping out the entire conversation I would have with John as if I alone would decide John's eternal destiny.

Boy, was I ever ready when our lunch rolled around that next week. My ducks were in a row, my guns were loaded and I was ready for anything. I was certain John Ogleton would walk into our meeting not knowing if God existed, but he would walk away from our meeting a new believer! My defense was strong, my points were clear and my logic was sound.

The day had arrived and as I parked my car in front of the restaurant I gathered my notes and my notepad off the passenger seat, tucked them under my arm and walked quickly into the restaurant. I asked the hostess for a booth and explained that my friend would be with us shortly. She led me to a quiet booth near the far corner of the busy restaurant. John showed up moments later.

I stood up to shake John's hand and as we sat down together John attempted to make small talk but I abruptly cut him off.

"John, I have a ton of stuff to tell you and we have a short time together so let's get started."

"Okay, Todd. What's up?"

As I spread my papers out in front of me I explained to John that I had been preparing for our meeting for some time, realizing that if I could only prove that the Bible was really created by God then he would be forced to accept its claim that Christ is the Savior of all men.

John, realizing at this point that he was not expected to be part of the ensuing "conversation" leaned back in his chair and politely listened.

"John, I found some amazing things over the past week about the Bible. First off," I turned my notepad around so he could follow along, "the Bible was written over a 1,500-year span, by over forty different authors, on three different continents, yet it comes together perfectly! It would be like picking sixty-six people at random from around this restaurant, assigning them each a chapter in a book, not telling them who was writing the chapter before or after theirs or what they were writing about, having them complete their chapters, putting the book together—and it making sense!"

John looked up as I paused. He smiled.

I went on.

"An atheist statistician claimed that it was not humanly possible for such a book to exist!"

I looked at John.

"Not humanly possible—no human could have orchestrated it!"

The waiter came to the table asking if we had time to look over our menus. John motioned for me to pause for a moment as he made his order. Then the waiter looked at me and I, being a bit rattled by the unexpected interruption of a waiter asking for my food order at a restaurant—where they served food—said, "I'm fine. No lunch today."

I turned the notepad around to retrace my steps, talking to myself.

"1,500 years, forty authors, three continents—the book thing—not humanly possible."

"Okay." I turned the notepad back toward John. "You'll be amazed by this. There are over 300—*three hundred* prophesies about Jesus in the Old Testament. They were written about his birth, life and even his death and resurrection. All of them were written centuries before he was born! Yet every single one of those 300 prophesies came true in the life of Jesus."

I looked up and almost certainly saw John's head nod slightly and I was nearly certain I saw him raise his eyebrows slightly. I took that as a good sign.

"I found an article that spoke of the statistical chances of even seven of the 300 prophesies coming true in the life of one man hundreds of years after they were written. The probability against this happening in the life of one man was a number greater than the stars in the known universe." I looked up at John who was still staring at the notepad. "John, there is no number large enough to define the odds of just seven prophesies coming true in the life of one man, let alone 300."

The waiter placed chips and hot sauce on the table along

with our drinks. John reached for a chip, looked at me and said simply.

"Interesting."

I took that as another good sign and continued.

"To top all of this compelling evidence, my final defense, I believe, is the most thought provoking. John, for over 2,000 years kings, rulers, politicians, scientists, atheists and agnostics have been trying to disprove the existence of even one war, one person or one claim in the Bible. The Bible itself claims to be the inerrant Word of God. Therefore, if even one iota of the Bible can be disproved, the reasoning goes, then the Bible would be proven errant and discounted completely. Yet, for 2,000 years not one person, war,

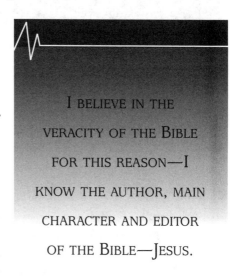

I BELIEVE IN THE VERACITY OF THE BIBLE FOR THIS REASON—I KNOW THE AUTHOR, MAIN CHARACTER AND EDITOR OF THE BIBLE—JESUS.

event or claim in the Bible has been disproved. Not one!"

This was the point in my notes where I believed the evidence presented to John would be so overwhelming, so irrefutable that he could do nothing but beg for forgiveness from his newfound Savior. Then the heavens were going to open up, a blinding light would shine on John, he would realize that God really did exist and he would become a child of God.

But ...

No parting of the clouds, no light shining down, nothing. John could see that my discourse was complete by the notes he was following on my outline. He looked up at me, smiled and took a drink of his recently mixed hot tea.

"Todd, I appreciate all the effort you put into this presentation.

This shows me you care about me and that means a lot to me. But I came to lunch today to hear your story, Todd. I wanted to hear the details of your experience as a Christian. I want to know what compelled you to literally discard twenty-four years of your life and choose to follow this path instead."

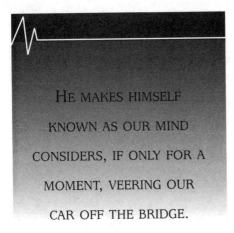

HE MAKES HIMSELF KNOWN AS OUR MIND CONSIDERS, IF ONLY FOR A MOMENT, VEERING OUR CAR OFF THE BRIDGE.

John's lunch plate came as he was explaining himself, and as he began to eat I was forced to ask myself an important question. Why did I decide after twenty-four years to discard my philosophy of life and choose to follow Jesus? Was it because Todd Riddle convinced me of the veracity of the Bible by giving me statistically irrefutable claims? My answer was no.

I watched as John began eating his lunch and realized that nothing I said regarding the Bible reached him at the core of his being. Statistics and reasoning were the foundation of John's life, yet he was looking for something beyond reason. He was looking for that which went beyond his education, insight and experience.

I had become too caught up in clearly detailing the points of my monologue to notice that John wanted something different. I played out the first few moments of our meeting in my mind and recalled words such as, "I came to hear your story" and "I want to hear the details of your experience" and "I want to know what compelled you." John gave me a recipe for success that day in the first moments of contact, but I chose not to listen. I missed those key phrases spoken from the mouth of a man searching for meaning.

Why did I believe the Bible was the Word of God? Why did

I count as Gospel the claims of Christ as Savior of the world? The answer didn't lie in the consideration of probabilities and statistics. Nor did it lie in the fact that even if the overwhelming evidence validating the claims of the Bible were presented in a court of law, any man could see that a judge would be forced to find for the Bible. No, my faith relied on a much simpler and more tactile experience. I believe in the veracity of the Bible for this reason—I know the author, main character, and editor of the Bible—Jesus. I had a personal, meaningful, and eternal relationship with veracity himself.

Ironically enough, I preached on the veracity of the Bible two years after my conversation with John and the response of the Christian audience was overwhelming! One by one they came, thanking me for "building them up in the faith." One young woman, reflecting upon her own salvation said suggestively, "What marvelous, encouraging and at the same time unnecessary information." Yet another said, "Todd, thank you for solidifying my faith in Jesus and reminding me that my pagan friends aren't as smart as they think they are."

To the believer, my apologetic defense of the Bible was like a perfect after-dinner mint. It was a sweet addition to the main course. Not a necessity, but a delightful and satisfying surprise. The meal would have been just as good without the mint. The main course would still have been "to die for."

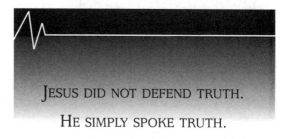

JESUS DID NOT DEFEND TRUTH.

HE SIMPLY SPOKE TRUTH.

My sermon was not necessary for their faith to survive, nor was it the appetizer upon which the entire meal garnered its worthiness. After all, how many believers have you met who give credit to rhetoric and reason for their faith in Jesus? There may be one or two, but the majority come to faith in Christ by, through, and in spite of brokenness, hopelessness, pain, and loss rather than wit, intellect, rhetoric, and reason.

We come to know Jesus by the stories of faith, the testimonies of our friends, family members, and even our enemies. We see the profound nature of God in the trials of life. We find him in the empty chair next to our hospital bed. He makes himself known as our mind considers, if only for a moment, veering our car off the bridge. He is the one who enters the room when everyone else is fleeing. He is the only one who stands vigil with us in our prayers to the Father. He is the one whom you find smiling at you from the courtroom gallery, somehow convincing you that life will go on after divorce. He gives the gift of peace to the infirm. He sits at the kitchen table in the middle of the night with those of us who find ourselves unable to sleep. He cries with us, for us and because of us.

I liken my relationship with Jesus to my relationship with my wife. First, I know Julie exists and I have a genuine relationship with her. No man or woman could ever convince me that she does not exist nor could they reason me out of my relationship with her. Secondly, my love for her has nothing to do with how others view her or her character. I simply know unwaveringly that Julie exists and that I am blessed to have a personal and meaningful relationship with her.

I'm not surprised when, after I have referred to my wife as an example in a sermon and spoken of her with words of fondness and affection, people come up to me and say, "I sure would like to meet your wife! She sounds like a lovely person." They are drawn to the story. They are drawn to my heartfelt prose about Julie's personality. They are drawn to the idea that they too might be able to experience the joy of time with my wife or that they might also find someone like my wife to live life with.

We must be diligent in our efforts to share with the world the story of our faith, the emotions of our trials and our victories with God and our experiences with the Creator of the

Universe. Doctrine is defended by apologetics. Jesus is offered through the narrative of our lives. Arguments do not win people to faith in Jesus. If anything, debate casts a dark shadow on the light that we offer.

There are some who have been brought to faith by apologetic discourse. Thomas, the doubting disciple, required empirical evidence that Jesus had, in fact, risen from the dead. For those who are wired this way, apologetics can be the very tool that God uses to make them alive together with Christ (Ephesians 2:5). But, for many of the apologists I have met, apologetics is not just one of many tools for witnessing; it is perceived as the only tool for evangelizing the unbeliever. This belief is as damaging to our cause as the idea that stadium evangelism is the only way to win souls. Jesus did not defend truth. He simply spoke truth. Jesus did not debate religion. He spoke in parable. The story was his primary form of communication. We must follow suit if we hope to "make disciples of all nations" (Matthew 28:19).

20

Developing Your
Evangelism Strategy

several years ago a good friend, Jeff Harris, the pastor of
Gracepoint Church in San Antonio, asked me to join his
staff for a time. He wanted desperately to develop a passion
for witnessing within the hearts of the church members. Jeff
has always been and will always be a true pastor/shepherd. On
the other hand, I am, and always will, have the heart of an apos-
tle and evangelist. He thought that I could bring something
unique to the church and I knew that Jeff could mentor me
personally, so I accepted his offer and began my service at
Gracepoint in late summer 2000. My task was simple—create
an all-encompassing strategy for evangelism that would per-
meate every heart in the congregation.

I occupied much of my time the first few months soaking up
the culture of the church. I talked to many people from many different areas of the church—from elders, to staff, to long-time
members and several visitors. After a few months I came to the

pastor with an evangelistic strategy for the church and we came to agreement on the wording of the vision statement that would define the church's vision for evangelism:

> One of the primary goals of Gracepoint Church is to help every member develop his or her own strategy for sharing the Gospel of Jesus Christ with the people with which they come in contact. Each member will develop this strategy based on his or her own God-given personality and spiritual gifts. Ultimately, every member will consistently develop and foster long-lasting relationships with non-Christians, having the ultimate hope of loving them into the Kingdom of God.

We then developed a strategy for achieving this vision. The strategy we outlined for Gracepoint Church is also a perfect strategy for any believer who really wants to get the ball rolling in this evangelistic discipline.

You Really Do Have a Story to Tell!

The first strategy had as its target the hearts of the new members. The church already required all prospective members to attend a new members class so we felt this was the most effective way to reach them. The purpose of the class was to help new and prospective members become familiar with the philosophy, doctrine, and vision of the church. The goal was not only to explain it in principle, but also to ultimately show how it was lived out in the life of the congregation, both individually and corporately.

Within this setting we simply added to the existing structure a lengthy section on the paramount importance of developing relationships with non-Christians. We used examples and stories relating to this topic throughout the class. Then we guided the prospective members through the process of developing their own testimonies, both on paper and orally. We made clear that our purpose for this activity was to equip them at the outset of their membership in the church with a written, well-thought-out testimony and a clear understanding of the unique and powerful features of their respective stories.

Our desire was to further the education of those involved by scripturally validating evangelism as an everyday opportunity for the believer coupled with the exercise of having them actually tell their story to someone else in the new members class. We believed strongly that the greatest barrier for most believers was the fear of sharing their salvation story for the first time in a clear way. If we could help them to get beyond the fear of their initial witnessing opportunity, they would be far more likely to share their faith in a real-world setting.

I remember one young man who was paired up with me at one of our new member classes to share his story. He seemed nervous and a bit apprehensive.

"Todd, I just don't have a story to tell."

"Has there been a point in your life where you asked Jesus to save you from your sins and take control of your life?"

"Yes, of course." He looked down at the ground as if he were embarrassed about something. "My story isn't like yours Todd. I was saved when I was seven years old. I never did anything wrong. I didn't take drugs or steal a car or go to jail. All I got forgiven for was throwing tantrums and stealing cookies. No one is going to listen to my story."

I paused for a moment with a big smile on my face, "John, that's the greatest story I've ever heard!"

Puzzled and with a

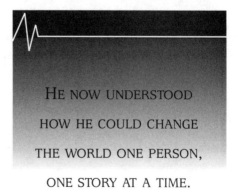

HE NOW UNDERSTOOD HOW HE COULD CHANGE THE WORLD ONE PERSON, ONE STORY AT A TIME.

look of disbelief, John asked, "What do you mean by that? Are you making fun of my silly testimony?"

"No, John. You don't understand. I didn't get to meet Jesus until I was twenty-four years old. I missed out on all of those years you had to get to know him—time you have been blessed to have with him! For me the greatest stories are ones just like yours. You *do* have a story to tell! The strength of your testimony is the fact that you have known Jesus for so much of your life, learned from him for so many years. Your story gives hope to guys like me who found Jesus later in life or who are looking for him right now at your office or on your softball team. Your story is truly remarkable!"

John's eyes lit up. He looked down again. Then he looked up with newfound energy. He was the first to share his testimony to the class. He shared his story with enthusiasm. An evangelist was born that day. Not necessarily a man who would speak to thousands at stadiums about Jesus, but—and perhaps more importantly—a man with the realization that he had a powerful story to tell. He knew he had a place in God's work on this earth. He now understood how he could change the world one person, one story at a time.

> I'VE HEARD IT SAID THAT YOU WILL ACCOMPLISH 30 PERCENT OF WHAT YOU THINK ABOUT DOING—BUT YOU WILL ACCOMPLISH 70 PERCENT OF WHAT YOU *WRITE* DOWN!

Many church members have very little confidence that their own salvation story has the power to compel someone to respond to God. Many believers have a very similar story to John, the young man I talked with in the new members class. Are you one of those believers? Have you, up until now, believed that your story wasn't worth telling? Well it is! The first suggestion I make to anyone who wants to know how to be more effective at sharing his or her faith is to write down his or her story. Then sit down with a friend, preferably a friend who is a more mature Christian, and begin to share the story with that friend, not just once but many times over several days. Get comfortable with the story that God gave you. Ask your partner what he or she feels are the strong points of your testimony. Then pray that God will give you the opportunity to share your story with someone who doesn't know God personally. You will find that your story is powerful and purposeful. Your confidence will soar!

Summary time—Write your story. Share it many times with a friend. Pray for opportunities to share your story with an unbeliever. When opportunity knocks, for God's sake, answer the door!

Personal Commitment

Another strategy we developed was very simple, but based on two important concepts: "Where there is no vision, the people perish" (Proverbs 29:18 KJV) and, "Write the vision and make it plain on tablets, that he may run who reads it" (Habakkuk 2:2 NKJV).

Our desire was to find a way for each church member to pray for and then write down clearly a vision for reaching those around them with the Good News. We developed a voluntary commitment card that each member could fill out. The commitment card simply stated that the person who signed the card would pray for at least one opportunity each year to share his or her faith. The cards were to be placed by the exit door so each member could, at his or her discretion, read and sign a card of commitment.

The reason was that our credo for evangelism in the church body was "opportunity rather than obligation." Never would we create a sense of obligation when it came to evangelism. We promoted evangelism as an opportunity that no Christian would want to miss. The cards were a form of self-accountability based on a person's own desire to develop a daily passion for evangelism.

I've heard it said that you remember 10 percent of what you hear, 30 percent of what you hear and read—but you remember 70 percent of what you hear, read, and *write down*! The same is true for accomplishment. I've heard it said that you will accomplish 30 percent of what you think about doing—but you will accomplish 70 percent of what you *write down*! How effective are you at goal setting? Do you have your one-, five- and ten-year goals written somewhere and do you reflect on them often? If you are like most, you do not have your personal, professional, or spiritual goals written in a clear manner. Without going on a tangent here, let me say that whoever put together the above statistics was on the money! Whether you are focusing on professional goals or witnessing goals you will likely not see the vision come to fruition unless you "write the vision and make it plain on tablets."

Summary time—Pray to God for a witnessing vision in your life. Write down the vision. Open your eyes and watch for God to work. Experience complete joy!

There's Nothing Like a Good Book

We also proposed to flood the church with opportunities for members to attend evangelism courses such as "Contagious Christianity" and others. Members would have opportunities to attend structured, biblically based courses to both educate and reiterate the ideas that were presented to them in the "New Christian" class.

In developing your personal evangelism strategy do you then wait for your church to offer a course on evangelism?

Certainly you should look at the church calendar to see if a course is available and take advantage of the opportunity to attend. Yet, more importantly, my plea is that you start now, with this book, developing a personal library of books that interest you about this topic. I've included a list of suggested reading relating directly to the subject of witnessing (appendix A).

Why is this so important? First, it keeps the concept of witnessing fresh in your mind. If you own a library of books on any subject and you pass by those books in your home regularly you can't help but think on the subject. Second, it gives you a tool for reference as you build new relationships with nonbelievers who have varied difficulties in life and varied backgrounds. Your library will enable you to draw from a wealth of information that will help you in your friendships with unbelievers. Third, in developing a library of works on any subject you have spent time and money creating it. It is now yours and you have as a result given value to your subject of interest. Fourth, if you have never pursued a topic in this manner or if the last time you read extensively on a specific subject was in high school or college, then my hope is that the discipline of developing this witnessing library will develop in you a habit. This habit of reading for the purpose of knowledge and life application will help you in every area of your life.

It Takes One to Know One

The final piece of our evangelistic strategy for Gracepoint was to change the paradigm of testimonies in the church services. Gracepoint and many of the churches I've attended make it a practice to have new Christians give their testimony during the Sunday service. I have always enjoyed the opportunity to hear what God has done in the lives of others. But I noticed a trend in every church I attended in relation to the people who were chosen to share their stories. Almost invariably the testimonies that were shared in the public forum were the extreme stories of drugs, alcohol, prostitution, prison, abortion and bankruptcies. They sounded like country/western songs. (Mine is one of these so I am not trying to trivialize the extreme nature of these testimonies.)

Another characteristic of these testimonies was often the extreme joy the individuals felt now, along with the lack of problems in their lives since meeting Jesus. It seemed as though life was hell before they met Jesus, but the day they met him everything in life became a bed of roses. I've alluded to this issue in previous chapters but I must address it specifically here. I am concerned about those who tell a story of moving from crisis to the sublime in the blink of an eye. As I said before, this creates false expectations in the minds of unbelievers. It gives credence to the idea that everything has to be perfect in your life as a Christian or something is wrong with you.

I cannot count the testimonies I've heard that follow this story line:

> I grew up in an abusive home. I was never popular in school. I got into drugs when I was in twelfth grade. I dropped out of high school, met a boy. I got pregnant and had an abortion. I started shoplifting to get money for my drugs. I was caught and spent eight months in jail. While I was in jail an inmate told me about Jesus and I asked Jesus to save me. *Ever since then my life has been perfect.*

That person is lying to the audience, lying to herself, or both! The Bible tells us repeatedly that, as Christians, we will certainly have trials of many kinds (James 1:2–3). Yet we parade these new believers, who have very little idea of the paramount reality of their newfound relationship with God, across our church stages to tell candy-coated stories of their salvation. This activity is potentially damaging to that new believer, the unbeliever in the audience and the mature believer who keeps hearing about all the perfect lives people have while they go through trials nearly every day!

In response to these two trends, I proposed that we begin to champion two types of stories:

1. The stories of the mature believers who have experienced both the peaks and the valleys of their relationships with God and lived to tell about the endurance, maturity and faith they have received through the trials of life, and

2. Testimonies from believers who share their faith with others! Not just the success stories of believers who are blessed with the ability to actually see a spiritually dead person become eternally alive in front of them, but the stories of believers who witness to others and get rejected.

These are the stories of the Christian life. My story is one of extreme sin and magnificent grace, but I still face trials every day. My story has no more impact for an audience than my wife's story of being saved at the age of seven and going through trials every day. I would argue that her story may be even more compelling to the masses because she represents longevity and certainty and long suffering and commitment to a much greater degree than I do as a younger believer.

For you this final strategy translates into finding one or two other believers in your life who might agree to take this evangelistic journey with you. They, too, have either read this book or another work on this topic of witnessing and possess the same passion as you do for unbelievers. You become for each other the inspiration through the trials of witnessing and the partner in celebration as you are afforded the opportunity to see someone breathe eternally for the first time. You must have someone who will share the peaks and the valleys with you to keep you grounded. So, what have we concluded?

1. Write your testimony down and then tell it to someone.
2. Pray to God for a witnessing vision in your life and write it down.
3. Develop a library of materials on the subject of evangelism.
4. Find a partner to share the peaks and valleys of your witnessing journey.

For those who buy in at this level, I promise a life much larger than you can possibly imagine!

21

Conclusion

All of what we have investigated to this point comes down to one thing—joy. Every person who has ever walked this earth, lives in our day, or is yet to be born, has been, is now, or will be existing with a dark, thick, and penetrating void in his life until he learns the secret of the universe—knowing God personally and finding joy in him forever.

We can guide our friends, family and even our enemies to the one true God of Abraham, Isaac, and Jacob. He has graciously allowed us to be part of the process of birthing people into his kingdom. And in volunteering to do his work we receive the gift of completed joy!

This one true God has revealed his character through his historic relationship with Israel.

This one true God has revealed his love for us by becoming a man and dwelling among us.

This one true God has revealed his grace by sending his Son to die for our sins.

This one true God has revealed his power by raising Jesus from the dead to be the firstborn among creation so that we might have eternal life.

This one true God has revealed his plan for us by using forty different authors on three different continents over 1,500 years to pen the words written in the Bible.

What a God we have! Share him with others. Give of yourself without expecting anything in return so that he can share his love with people who don't yet know him. Pray that God will reveal to you your own evangelistic strategy, custom made for your life circumstances. Read. Pray. Love. Hope. Seek. Find. Trust.

Appendix A

Resources for Evangelism

Web Sites

WWW.BARNA.ORG—The official site of George Barna, one of the preeminent evangelical researchers of our time.

WWW.NAVIGATORS.ORG—Great organization for discipleship training and evangelism resources.

WWW.CCCI.ORG—Campus Crusade for Christ International is a global organization dedicated to sharing the Gospel around the world. The resources on this site are exceptional evangelistic tools.

WWW.EVANGELISMTOOLBOX.COM—Top site for evangelistic resources and links to other evangelistic sites.

WWW.EEINTERNATIONAL.ORG—Dr. D. James Kennedy's web site for Evangelism Explosion.

Books to Build Your Evangelism Library

Master Plan of Evangelism. Robert Coleman. (Revell)

Jesus For a New Generation. Kevin Graham Ford. (InterVarsity Press)

The Embarrassed Believer. Hugh Hewitt. (Word)

Becoming a Contagious Christian. Bill Hybels, Mark Mittelberg. (Zondervan)

Out of the Salt Shaker & Into the World. Rebecca Manley Pippert. (InterVarsity Press)

Books to Be Read and Given to Seeking Friends

Mere Christianity. C. S. Lewis. (Touchstone)

Alone in the Universe? David Wilkinson. (InterVarsity Press)

Basic Christianity. John Stott. (InterVarsity Press)

Letters From a Skeptic. Dr. Gregory A. Boyd, Edward K. Boyd. (Victor/Cook Communications)

Appendix B

Gospel Outlines

ROMAN ROAD

The following Gospel presentation is one that I have given hundreds of times in both private settings as well as public events. The core of the presentation is based on four passages from the book of Romans. These passages are called the "Roman Road" and have been used by many organizations including the Southern Baptist Convention and Campus Crusade for Christ in one form or another to present the Gospel in a clear way. The following is a variation on many of the presentations that I have seen and heard. I've used this presentation to speak primarily to the younger generations ranging in age from 12 to 35 years.

Presentation

The Bible makes it very clear that every person has sinned against God. *Sinning* is a term God uses to describe even one decision in a person's life that goes against God's truth.

"For all have sinned and fall short of the glory of God" (Romans 3:23).

The Bible also shows us that because each one of us has sinned, we are in a state of being eternally separated from God.

"For the wages of sin is death ... " (Romans 6:23).

But God has a plan for each and every person to be able to live forever with him.

"... but, the gift of God is eternal life through Jesus Christ" (Romans 6:23 KJV).

As you can see, God's plan was for his Son, Jesus Christ, to enable all men to receive a free gift from God—eternal life! How did he make this possible? He sent his Son, Jesus, to die for our sins so that we wouldn't have to pay the penalty for sin in our life.

"But God demonstrates his own love for us in this: While we were still sinners, Christ died for us" (Romans 5:8).

You see, God didn't demand that we get our act together or become religious before he would accept us. In fact, according to the above passage, the way God decided to show us the depth of his love was to save us from our sin while we were still sinning!

So, how do you meet this loving God who wants to have a personal relationship with you that lasts forever? He didn't get us all the way to this point to leave us hanging when it comes to the *how!* In another Bible passage God tells us:

"That if you confess with your mouth, 'Jesus is Lord,' and believe in your heart that God raised him from the dead, you will be saved" *(Romans 10:9).*

Now, let me give you a word of caution. It's not enough just to say these words. This is not some magical chant that, if said in the proper order, forces God to let you into heaven. In fact, if you say these words but they mean nothing in your heart then they are empty.

But, if you are reading this and thinking "if God is real and he wants to have a relationship with me that lasts forever, I want to meet him too!" then all you have to do is talk to God. Speak to him from your heart. Read the following prayer and if you understand what it says and want God to forgive you and start a relationship with you that is real, personal and eternal then say those words to God, meaning them sincerely in your heart and God will be faithful to forgive you!

"If we confess our sins, he is faithful and just and will forgive us our sins and purify us from all unrighteousness" *(1 John 1:9).*

Tell this to God:

> "God, I don't know you but I want to know you.
> I realize now that I can know you personally.
> I accept Jesus' payment for my sins and ask you to forgive me.

> Please start a relationship with me right now that lasts forever.
> Thank you for making me a child of God today."

BRIDGE TO LIFE

Step 1—God's Love and His Plan

God created us in his own image to be his friend and to experience a full life assured of his love, abundant and eternal.

> Jesus said, "... I have come that they may have life, and have it to the full" (John 10:10).

> "... we have peace with God through our Lord Jesus Christ" (Romans 5:1).

Since God planned for us to have peace and abundant life right now, why are most people not having this experience?

Step 2—Our Problem: Separation from God

God created us in his own image to have abundant (meaningful) life. He did not make us robots to automatically love and obey him, but he gave us a will and a freedom of choice.

We chose to disobey God and go our own willful way. We still make this choice today. This results in separation from God.

> "For all have sinned and fall short of the glory of God" (Romans 3:23).

> "... your iniquities have separated you from your God; your sins have hidden his face from you, so that he will not hear" (Isaiah 59:2).

On our own, there's no way we can attain the perfection needed to bridge the gap to God. Through the ages, individuals have tried many ways ... without success.

Good works won't do it ... or religion ... or money ... or morality ... or philosophy ... "There is a way that seems right to a man, but in the end it leads to death" (Proverbs 14:12).

Step 3—God's Remedy: The Cross

Jesus Christ is the only answer to this problem. He died on the cross and rose from the grave, paying the penalty for our sin and bridging the gap between God and people.

"For Christ died for sins once for all, the righteous for the unrighteous, to bring you to God." (1 Peter 3:18).

"For there is one God and one mediator between God and men, the man Christ Jesus" (1 Timothy 2:5).

"But God demonstrates His own love for us in this: While we were still sinners, Christ died for us" (Romans 5:8).

Step 4—Our Response

Believing means trust and commitment—acknowledging our sinfulness, trusting Christ's forgiveness and letting him control our life. Eternal, abundant life is a gift for us to receive.

> "For God so loved the world that he gave his one and only son, that whoever believes in him shall not perish but have eternal life" (John 3:16).

> "I tell you the truth, whoever hears my word and believes him who sent me has eternal life and will not be condemned; he has crossed over from death to life" (John 5:24).

Is there any reason why you shouldn't cross over to God's side and be certain of eternal life?

How to Receive Christ:

1. Admit your need (I am a sinner).
2. Be willing to turn from your sins (repent).
3. Believe that Jesus Christ died for you on the cross and rose from the grave.
4. Through prayer, invite Jesus Christ to come in and control your life through the Holy Spirit (Receive him as Lord and Savior of your life).

What to Pray

Dear Lord Jesus,

I know that I am a sinner and need your forgiveness. I believe that you died for my sins. I want to turn from my sins. I now invite you to come into my heart and life. I want to trust and follow you as the Lord and Savior of my life.

In your name. Amen.

God's Assurance of Eternal Life

If you've prayed this prayer and are trusting Christ, then the Bible says that you can be sure you have eternal life.

"... for, 'Everyone who calls on the name of the Lord will be saved'" (Romans 10:13).

"For it is by grace you have been saved, through faith—and this not from yourselves, it is the gift of God—not by works, so that no one can boast" (Ephesians 2:8–9).

"He who has the Son has life; he who does not have the Son of God does not have life. I write these things to you who believe in the name of the Son of God so that you may know that you have eternal life" (1 John 5:12–13).

Receiving Christ, we are born into God's family through the supernatural work of the Holy Spirit who indwells every believer ... this is called regeneration or the "new birth."

What Next?

This is just the beginning of a wonderful new life in Christ. To deepen this relationship you should:

1. Maintain regular intake of the Bible to know Christ better.
2. Talk to God in prayer every day.
3. Tell others about your new faith in Christ.
4. Worship, fellowship and serve with other Christians in a church where Christ is preached.
5. As Christ's representative in a needy world, demonstrate your new life by your love and concern for others.

Used by permission of NavPress, Colorado Springs, CO.
All rights reserved.
For more information, check out the *Bridge to Life* booklet at
www.navpress.com.

ONE-VERSE EVANGELISM
How to Share Christ's Love Conversationally & Visually
by Randy D. Raysbrook

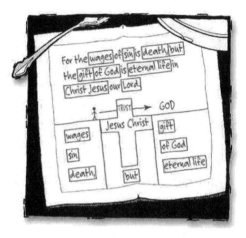

Many people feel that to be effective in evangelism they must memorize a complex illustration and a multitude of verses. But the Gospel is most powerful when shared with love, clarity, and simplicity. One-Verse Evangelism® is a simple, interactive way to share Christ's love conversationally and visually. It is based on asking questions and sharing. It's easy to learn because it uses just one verse. One-Verse Evangelism® is also sensitive to peoples' busy schedules because it can be shared in just 10 or 15 minutes. Here's a brief look at how it works. Let's say God's leading you to share the Gospel with your neighbor, Jeff. Write out Romans 6:23 on a piece of paper or a napkin: "For the wages of sin is death, but the gift of God is eternal life in Christ Jesus our Lord." Then put your Bible away. Ask Jeff if he would like to see a simple picture based on this verse that will explain God's relationship with people.

Circle this word and ask, "How would you feel if your boss refused to pay you the wages that were due to you?" Deep down, we all know that it is only right that we get what we deserve.

Similarly, we earn wages from God for how we have lived our lives.

Draw a circle around "sin," asking your friend what he thinks when he hears this word. You might explain that sin is more an attitude than an action. It can be either actively fighting God or merely excluding Him from our lives. You can ask, "Has God ever seemed far away?" If he says yes, let him know that's one of the things sin does—it makes God seem far away. Now draw two opposing cliffs with a gap in between.

Circle this word and ask what thoughts come to mind. Explain that death in the Bible always means some kind of separation.

While circling this word, mention that it is important because it means that a sharp contrast in thought is coming. What we have just looked at is bad news; what follows is good news.

Draw a circle around this word. Ask, "If wages are what a person earns, then what is a gift?" Remind your friend that someone must purchase every gift.

of God

Circle this and explain that the gift you are talking about is free. It is from God himself. It's so special that no one else can give it. Ask, "How do you feel when someone gives you a special gift?"

eternal life

Circle these two words next, and then ask, "How would you define these words?" Contrast one side of the cliff, death, with the other side, eternal life. Ask, "What is the opposite of separation from God?"

Christ Jesus

Draw these words so they create a bridge between the two cliffs. Help your friend to consider that every gift has a giver, and only Jesus Christ can give the gift of eternal life.

TRUST

Write this word over the bridge you just drew. Explain that friends trust each other, and tell your friend that Jesus wants a trusting friendship with him. All he has to do is admit that he is responsible for the "sin" of either fighting or excluding God from his life. That is what trust means—trusting that Jesus wants to forgive us for rejecting him from our lives. At this point, you can ask him if he wants to start a relationship with God that will last forever. If he says "Yes," invite him to pray a short prayer in his own words, asking Jesus to forgive him. Close by reminding him that this simple illustration shows what God is like: someone who really cares about people, especially him. Invite him to read all about it in the Bible, perhaps beginning in the gospel of John.

Adapted with permission from *One-Verse Evangelism*, © 2000 Randy D. Raysbrook. All rights reserved. To order the booklet, contact Dawson Media at www.dawsonmedia.com, call (719) 594-2100, or write to Dawson Media, a ministry of The Navigators, P.O. Box 6000, Colorado Springs, CO 80934.

Contact the author of *Spiritual CPR*:

WWW.TODDPHILLIPS.NET
46 Courtside Circle
San Antonio, Texas 78216
(210) 887-4500
mail@toddphillips.net

Reader's Guide

For Personal Reflection
or Group Discussion

Introduction to Reader's Guide

Have you ever witnessed someone having a heart attack? If so, did time seem suddenly to stand still? In those short, critical moments when life hung in the balance, were you frozen in place—wishing you were able to help, that you had taken the time to learn what to do in a situation like this one? Or were you prepared and ready to respond—leaping into action to save a life?

Whether we realize it or not, people are in crisis all around us. Every day we come in contact with individuals who need intervention—someone to step in and revive their dying hearts. We've all been there. Ephesians 2:1 says, "As for you, you were dead in your transgressions and sins, in which you used to live when you followed the ways of this world." Do you remember what it was like to live without hope? What did it feel like to suddenly have life breathed into your spirit?

As believers, we can experience complete joy by obeying Jesus' command to reach the lost. But in order to be successful, we must be ready. We must not be hindered by selfishness, apathy, or

Based upon your personal experience and observation, is it true that two-thirds of Christians today do not share their faith? What does the term "witnessing" mean to you? In what ways do you currently have opportunity to share the good news of Christ with others as a part of your daily routine?

fear. To be effective at saving lives we have to be obedient to the leading of the Holy Spirit, and we must be trained.

As you consider the following questions, ask God to begin to change your heart and teach you. Pray that he will open your spiritual eyes and set you free from anything that holds you back from sharing the love of Christ with others. Ask him for wisdom. And finally, ask him for help—that he would open doors of influence, that you will make the most of every opportunity, and that you will lovingly communicate the message of Christ in all of its power, mercy, and grace.

Remember that Jesus said, "You are the light of the world. A city on a hill cannot be hidden. Neither do people light a lamp and put it under a bowl. Instead they put it on its stand, and it gives light to everyone in the house. In the same way, let your light shine before men, that they may see your good deeds and praise your Father in heaven" (Matthew 5:14–16). As you step out in obedience and faith to help those in crises of the spirit, you will surely fulfill the greatest calling on your life.

Study Guide Questions for Spiritual CPR
CHAPTER ONE
WHAT'S YOUR COVER?

1. Based upon your personal experience and observation, is it true that two-thirds of Christians today do not share their faith? What does the term "witnessing" mean to you? In what ways do you currently have opportunity to share the good news of Christ with others as a part of your daily routine?

2. What do you think the old man meant when he said that his mop and bucket were his "cover"? How about you? What cover opportunities has God placed in your life? Does it alter your perspective any to consider that your

job, activities, or other social commitments may serve a higher purpose?

3. Do Christians really fail to witness because they don't know *why* they should? What other issues can contribute to a believer's reluctance to share the Gospel? Are any of these issues influential in your own life?

4. Jesus said to his disciples, "Go into all the world and preach the good news to all creation" (Mark 16:15). Why aren't we sufficiently motivated to obey God's commandment, whether or not we know why?

5. Have you ever been asked to complete a task without being told why you were doing it? When you are given greater understanding, does that make the task somewhat less tedious? Why or why not? Is there a greater blessing for those believers who place their confident trust in God's wisdom and simply obey without questioning?

CHAPTER TWO
THE TERRIBLE TWOS

1. Many people—believers and nonbelievers alike—quickly respond to the notion of getting "something for nothing." Do some Christians view their salvation as a "free ride"? While salvation cannot be earned and is a free work of grace, are there inherent responsibilities and consequences for the decision to become a disciple of Christ?

2. What do you think about the statement that "many of us are stunted in our spiritual growth and we think it's normal"? Have you witnessed examples of "mature" Christians who are still trapped in the "terrible twos" of their faith? Why do

some Christians grow in maturity and wisdom while others seem to become stagnant?

3. Jesus spent most of his time with the dregs of society—outcasts, prostitutes, tax collectors, and worse. How did Jesus respond to the unclean? Did he seek to receive something from those who followed him, or did he seek to serve them? In what ways can we follow his example?

4. Why do so many Christians try to avoid mingling with the world? How has this attitude infiltrated the church? Are we fulfilling our role as the body of Christ if we segregate ourselves from those who need Jesus most? Is your church a spiritual country club or a holy hospital? How does your congregation respond to someone who seems different or who doesn't fit in?

CHAPTER THREE
GIVING ALL YOU'VE GOT

1. What was the significance of Jesus' final instructions to his disciples? Why did he tell them to make disciples, baptize, and teach, rather than something more profound or spiritual? Do you think the disciples would have preferred a more personal message of farewell and encouragement?

2. Throughout Jesus' ministry on earth, the disciples continuously demonstrated their weaknesses, failures, and humanness. Is it likely the disciples doubted their ability to effectively disciple others for Christ? What insights can be found in 1 Corinthians 1:27 and 2 Corinthians 12:7–9? What do these scriptures tell us about our own inadequacies?

3. Why didn't the disciples immediately leap into action once

they realized that Jesus was alive and well? How do you think it felt to be reunited with Jesus, only to have him leave so quickly? Do you think seeing Jesus ascend into heaven had any effect on the disciples' fear of sharing their faith?

4. What prospect do you think intimidated the disciples more—witnessing in Jerusalem or at the "ends of the earth"? Why is it usually more difficult to share the Gospel with those closest to us? What personal limitations do you think might hinder you from spreading the Gospel around the world?

CHAPTER FOUR
TOTAL DEVOTION

1. Why do you think Jesus entrusted his ministry to eleven imperfect men—rather than an army of followers? What was Jesus able to see in each of his disciples that they didn't even realize themselves? What does this reveal about what God can accomplish in your own life if you are willing to give him everything?

2. Under the Old Testament law, or old covenant, God required that his people sacrifice the very best they possessed. They were to give the first fruits of the crop or a perfect, unblemished animal—otherwise it was an affront to God. What does God expect from us now as New Testament believers? What insight does Hebrews 13:15 give us as to what God desires most in our worship? Is it likely that he no longer wants the "best" we have to give?

3. In the book of Genesis, Cain and Abel each made their sacrifice of worship to God. Cain obediently offered the very first fruits of his crop—so why did God not look with favor

on the offering? Was God rejecting Cain's offering, or the secret attitudes of his heart? (See Genesis 4:3–7.) What important lesson from Cain's example can we apply today?

4. Why do you think so many Christians have developed a "show time" concept of worship? Have you ever found yourself critiquing a worship service you have attended? What is God more likely to critique—the excellence of the "show," or the quality of our hearts? (See Ezekiel 33:31 and Matthew 15:8–9.)

CHAPTER FIVE
LIVES LIVED ON THE TAKE

1. The kingdom of God is famous for paradoxes—and a significant one is that only by freely giving our lives away will we receive the desires of our hearts. How is this possible? Luke 6:38 says, "Give, and it will be given to you. A good measure, pressed down, shaken together and running over, will be poured into your lap. For with the measure you use, it will be measured to you." What are examples in your own life when you blessed someone generously, only to have God bless you in return beyond what you thought possible?

2. Malachi 3:10 says, "'Bring the whole tithe into the storehouse, that there may be food in my house. Test me in this,' says the Lord Almighty, 'and see if I will not throw open the floodgates of heaven and pour out so much blessing that you will not have room enough for it.'" Even though this passage is specifically referencing giving our money to God, what is the key lesson that is being taught? How can we test God in other areas of our lives?

3. When you consider your personal relationships and commitments, do you think that you are living a life "on the take"? In what practical ways can you practice the art of giving? How is evangelism the ultimate example of blessing others?

4. Philippians 4:19 tells us, "And my God will meet all your needs according to his glorious riches in Christ Jesus." If we choose to stop worrying about ourselves and focus on the needs of others, can we trust God to take care of us? Is it possible to "out give" God?

CHAPTER SIX
YOUR VERY OWN SPIRITUAL FOUNTAIN OF YOUTH

1. What is the difference between real joy and happiness? Which experience does the world seek after? How does sharing the truth about Jesus with others make our joy complete?

2. What do you remember most about your salvation experience? Do you still have the same level of passion and commitment that you did then? How have your feelings changed since you first came to know Christ?

3. Why are Christians so reluctant to admit that they are struggling with problems or have become spiritually stagnant? Who really benefits from the masks we wear for each other? What might happen if you were to become completely transparent and honest with a trusted friend?

4. Have you ever heard yourself say or thought to yourself, "I do everything in my relationship with God but witness"? How can missing just one aspect of our Christian life—like evangelism—have a devastating effect on our Christian

walk? Is witnessing a more important ingredient than other aspects of a godly life?

5. What are the differences between the gift of evangelism and the call to evangelize? If we don't have the gift, are we excused from sharing our faith? Why or why not?

CHAPTER SEVEN
SPIRITUAL CPR

1. When you think about the concept of people who are "spiritually dead," who comes to mind? What characterizes their life without God? Are there people in this condition that you could be reaching with the hope of Christ—family members, coworkers, friends, acquaintances, and neighbors?

2. If you were to encounter a homeless person who was desperately in need of food and clothing, or a child who was hurt and needed urgent medical care, how would you respond? Why are we usually more willing to meet urgent physical needs rather than spiritual ones? Is the state of a person's soul any less important than their physical condition?

3. Many people believe that they are not only responsible to witness, but that God also expects them to achieve a "positive" result. Is this a realistic expectation? Is it true that our joy is made complete simply by sharing the Gospel—not only by assuring a person's salvation? If so, does this understanding change your outlook on the importance of sharing the Good News?

4. Have you ever felt as though you failed if an individual

didn't respond positively to your witness? Have you been hesitant to speak openly about Jesus in the past because you feared a negative outcome? Why would Satan want to encourage your doubts and fears? Does it help to consider that we are only responsible to plant seeds, while God is responsible to bring about the harvest?

5. Rarely is one person's influence sufficient to lead someone to salvation. In most cases, it is the result of many faithful Christians and the cumulative efforts of many seeds that lead people to a saving knowledge of Christ. What does Paul have to say about this subject in 1 Corinthians 3:4–9? Is there a danger in starting to believe that we do the saving?

CHAPTER EIGHT
"THAT'S MY COVER"

1. Many people today—Christians included—spend their whole lives pursuing success, wealth, or fame in their chosen careers. Do you think we try so hard to succeed at our "cover" that we fail to carry out our true assignment? Why or why not?

2. Whether we labor in a Christian ministry or in the secular market, we all face challenges on the job. Do you ever find yourself complaining about your work environment? Do you have a difficult boss, unpleasant coworkers, or unfair pay? Have you come under unjust attack or even been persecuted for your faith? What does the Bible have to say about how we should respond to these types of situations? (See Matthew 10:22; Luke 6:22–23, 27–31; John 16:33; James 1:2–4, 12; 2 Thessalonians 1:3–4; John 9:4–5; Colossians 3:23–24.)

3. Has God really placed many of us in dark and hopeless

surroundings simply because we are his children? What hope should that give us? What did Paul mean when he said that we are Christ's ambassadors? (See 2 Corinthians 5:17–21.) What are the unique qualifications and responsibilities of an ambassador and how can you accomplish them for Christ on a daily basis?

4. Are all of life's circumstances really providential opportunities to share the Gospel? What different approach can you take on the job, with an unpleasant neighbor, or when waiting in the incredibly slow checkout lane at the grocery store? What difference might it make if we always kept our "lights" on? What unseen consequences can result when we choose not to share the truth or allow God's love to shine through us?

5. If you were to compare your life to the analogy of a sandwich, what ingredient would define you? Is Christ the central focus of your being or do other desires and pursuits take first priority? What does Matthew 7:15–27 reveal about what waits for those who call themselves believers but whose actions do not match their words?

CHAPTER NINE
FOR JOY TO BE COMPLETE, IT MUST BE SHARED

1. When you accomplish something great in your life or you have wonderful news to tell, what is usually the first thing you want to do? Are there any people that you just have to call and share your good news with? How should this same principle apply to sharing the Good News of our faith?

2. A relatively new concept in communication is that we each have our own "love language," or the means by which we are

most effectively assured of someone's concern and devotion. Some people respond best to words of encouragement and edification ("tell me you love me"), others to acts of service ("show me you love me"). Is it true that "God's love language is obedience?" What significant role does obedience play in winning the lost?

3. Do you clearly remember your own salvation experience? Does the word "joy" aptly capture the emotion of that moment? What do you think David meant when he asked God to "restore to me the joy of your salvation"? (See Psalm 51:12.)

4. Do you remember asking your parents "why" when you were a child? Did you like it when they inevitably responded, "Because I said so!"? Did you think that if they were going to make you do something, they should at least explain why? Does God, as our heavenly parent, always explain everything he wants us to do? Does he ever command us to do something, for no other reason than because he told us to do it? Is this a good enough reason to obey? What role does faith play in helping us obey? (See Hebrews 11:1–6.)

CHAPTER TEN
PEOPLE MATTER

1. Matthew 10:29–31 says, "Are not two sparrows sold for a penny? Yet not one of them will fall to the ground apart from the will of your Father. And even the very hairs of your head are all numbered. So don't be afraid; you are worth more than many sparrows." What does this tell us about the value God places on the life of each and every one of us? By contrast, in this age of widespread abortion, "mercy

killings," human embryo and cloning experimentation, what value does the world place on human life?

2. What do you think Jesus meant when he said, "whatever you did for one of the least of these, you did for me"? (See Matthew 25:35–36, 40). What does this reveal about the heart of God toward his people? In what tangible ways can you serve "the least" in your own life?

3. How can a deeper realization of the truth that people matter help us to understand the *why* of evangelism? Can you think of a better way to show your gratitude to Jesus for saving you?

CHAPTER ELEVEN
WHY DOES GOD LOVE ME?

1. Do you ever have trouble believing that you are really God's "treasured creation"? Do you find it difficult to understand how God can love you even after you've done so many bad things? What does Romans 5:1–11 say about the subject?

2. Have you ever avoided witnessing to someone who seems to have everything—simply assuming they are not open to the Gospel? Is this a form of "spiritual snobbery"? Jesus said, "It is hard for a rich man to enter the kingdom of heaven" (Matthew 19:23). How is this truth apparent in our society today? Are we as believers offering an effective solution to the problem or contributing to it?

3. What do you think about the concept that all sin is equal? Does it seem just and fair that "sin is sin"—whether you tell a lie, lose your temper, or gossip about a friend, your sins are no different in God's sight than those of a murderer, drug

addict, or prostitute? Why should this be a source of joy, rather than a point of bitterness and division?

4. The church today has some striking inconsistencies when it comes to dealing with sin. How often do leaders fall into sexual immorality—among other things—only for the issue to be swept under the rug? One wife is replaced with another and we are told we should "forgive and forget." Yet these same churches refuse to welcome people who don't fit in properly, particularly if they are struggling with serious issues such as alcoholism, drug addiction, homosexuality, or abuse. How has this attitude of unpardonable sin affected the church's ability to evangelize the lost?

5. Why is it so important to personally experience God's love, rather than just having an intellectual understanding of it? Is it possible to give something away if we don't possess it ourselves?

6. How can understanding God's heart revolutionize how we approach witnessing? What has the greater appeal for the unbeliever—relationship or religion? What role does justice play in the Good News? How do grace, mercy, and unconditional love set the message of Christ apart from every other world religion? (See Psalm 117:2; Romans 2:1–11; Romans 3:21–26; Matthew 9:13; Ephesians 2:1–5; Titus 3:3–7; 2 Peter 3:9.)

CHAPTER TWELVE
THE PRICELESS VALUE OF ONE INDIVIDUAL TO GOD

1. Why is it significant that God is the source of all true passion? Is it accurate to say that "if you search for passion in life

you will inevitably find God"? Are there sincerely passionate people who do not eventually find God? Why or why not?

2. Why is it so much easier to give ourselves to a group or specific cause, rather than sharing in the suffering and misery of individual people? Have you experienced this in your own life? How is loving one the more difficult and complicated undertaking?

3. What personal application can you draw from the parable of the one? Do you identify most with the sheep who has gone astray, or the ninety-nine left in the fold? What challenges have you faced in your life, and how do they color your view of the other sheep?

4. Most of us do not have difficulty storming the gates of heaven for our relatives and friends who need to know God, but we are much less likely to exert equal energy on behalf of those who cause us trouble or heartache. Are we missing the best opportunities God has for us because of this type of attitude? How can we justify ignoring our responsibility to those God has called us to minister to—whether or not we like them?

CHAPTER THIRTEEN
GETTING PRACTICAL: WHAT IS THE RESULT OF OUR MISUNDERSTANDING?

1. Many of us grew up with the assumption that going on the mission field meant giving up everything familiar to serve in desolate places at the ends of the earth, such as Africa or Asia. People there, we told ourselves, really need the Gospel of Christ! Were you surprised to learn that America is now considered one of the greatest mission fields on earth? Does

it shock you that other countries send their missionaries here? What does this tell us about the potential impact we can have on the mission field—without ever leaving our own backyard?

2. How has America, which was founded by believers and established on Christian principles, evolved from "one nation, under God" to a post-Christian society? Are we in any way responsible for the dramatic changes that have come about in our culture? Has our relative silence made the popular humanistic, New Age religions more attractive to those seeking truth?

3. Is it true that most churchgoers in America today are biblically illiterate? Could this be the reason that the younger generations see the church as increasingly irrelevant and lacking legitimate answers to life's problems? How has the American church allowed itself to become so impotent?

4. With so many false gospels circulating in our world today— many blatantly claiming to be "Christian"—how do we learn to discern truth from deception? Have you ever struggled with determining if a book or television show is dealing truthfully with Scripture or not? What did Jesus mean when he said that his sheep would recognize his voice? (See John 10:1–16.)

5. How can we effectively compete with the polished and persuasive deceptions of the world? Do we need to become more spiritually savvy in order to effectively witness for Christ? Does it encourage you to know that God has deliberately chosen "foolish" things to confound those who think they are wise? What comfort can we take in the scripture,

"My grace is sufficient for you, for my power is made perfect in weakness" (2 Corinthians 12:9)?

6. According to John 14:6, what's wrong with the politically correct notion that there are many spiritual paths that lead to heaven? Why are we so willing to change the message in order to try and make it more attractive to people? Are we really concerned that people will reject Christ, or do we fear personal rejections?

CHAPTER FOURTEEN
BE LOYAL NO MATTER WHAT!

1. Loyalty is a term that is often overused and underachieved in today's world. Have you ever felt betrayed by someone who promised to be faithful to you? How rare is true loyalty, and how might that effectively reach people who have only known loss, rejection, abandonment, and abuse?

2. What characterizes godly loyalty? How does Jesus' commitment to Peter even in the face of betrayal provide us with hope, direction, and strength to follow his example? What might God be able to accomplish through us if we were to willingly pour out our lives for others—without any expectation of something in return?

3. Todd Riddle was completely unaware of the effectiveness of his testimony. From his perspective, he wasn't making any progress at all. How might the outcome have been different if he had given up or refused to make himself available? How does the example of Todd Riddle's witness illustrate the importance of building relationship when reaching the lost?

4. Isaiah 55:11 says, "So is my word that goes out from my mouth: It will not return to me empty, but will accomplish what I desire and achieve the purpose for which I sent it." How can we learn to sow seeds in the lives of others and trust God to accomplish his purpose? Why is it so important to remain full of faith and not rely on what we think we see in the natural?

CHAPTER FIFTEEN
LISTEN ... NO, I MEAN REALLY LISTEN!

1. Have you ever struggled with feeling as though no one listens to what you have to say or really understands you? Is it an accurate description to say that people who don't listen have a disease of the heart? Is it possible to hear someone talk without ever really understanding what they are saying?

2. Do you think that many Christians are too quick to speak—joyfully declaring all of their blessings and victories with great enthusiasm? Why is it that these well-intentioned proclamations are unlikely to be received or understood by someone who doesn't know Jesus? Is it possible that our zeal could turn people off before they have an opportunity to experience the truth of God's grace for themselves? How can we become less focused on ourselves and more aware of the needs of others?

3. Why is it so important to offer encouragement to unbelievers, even when they are living in sin? Do you find it difficult to support an individual without encouraging their sin? What is the difference between sympathy and empathy? Why is it important to discover their "misery factor" and "feel their pain"?

Spiritual CPR

4. What are the advantages of friendship evangelism? What does it mean to earn the right to be heard? How will most people respond if they sense any insincerity or wrong motives?

5. Many times, we only reach out to our un-churched neighbors to invite them to the Easter Pageant at church or the crusade that is coming to town. Do you think that they will believe you care about their eternal destiny if you don't respond to their everyday problems? How can we show God's love in practical ways that meet people at their point of need? If we fail to be like Jesus in the small things, what effect might this have on their opinion of Christianity?

CHAPTER SIXTEEN
FOR GOD'S SAKE, DON'T CANDY-COAT THE GOSPEL

1. Do you think it is an accurate statement that most Christians and churches today offer a candy-coated Gospel? Is it an honest representation of the life of faith to tell unbelievers only about the emotional highs and blessings of following Christ? Can this approach backfire? Do we really have a responsibility to warn new Christians of the storm before the calm? Why or why not?

2. Tony Campolo, a well-known Christian author and speaker, once said, "If we lose this present generation of young people, it will not be because we made the Gospel too difficult; it will be because we made the Gospel way too easy." What do you think he meant by that?

3. Why is it so important for a new believer to have realistic expectations of his or her new relationship with Christ? Were you sufficiently prepared for the trials that came early

in your walk with God? How can our honesty and transparency serve to help birth legitimate, unswerving commitments for Christ?

4. Do you agree that the most important thing we should tell the unbeliever is to expect Jesus to enter their "temple" and clean house? Is the new believer sure to face a time of struggle and upheaval? Why or why not?

5. Are there other forces at work that can cause trouble in a new believer's life? First Peter 5:8–9 says, "Your enemy the devil prowls around like a roaring lion looking for someone to devour. Resist him, standing firm in the faith, because you know that your brothers throughout the world are undergoing the same kind of sufferings." We know the angels rejoice, but how does Satan respond to the salvation of a soul? Is he content to lose his prey without a fight? How can preparing new Christians for the battles ahead prevent distrust and disillusionment—even spiritual death?

CHAPTER SEVENTEEN
GETTING SOMETHING VS. BECOMING SOMEONE

1. Were you surprised to read that many of the invitations for salvation offered in our churches every week are flawed? Do you agree that just telling someone they can have an address in heaven and that God will forgive their sins is an incomplete Gospel? Why is the offer of a "Get Out of Hell Free" card not sufficient to truly change the hearts of unbelievers?

2. Many people in the world have a "live for today, for tomorrow we die" mentality. Even those who call out to God on their deathbed are offered forgiveness and the hope of

heaven—so why shouldn't we all just live it up and wait until we are about to die to call on God? How do we convince people that they really should commit their life to Christ now, forsaking the passions and desires of the world?

3. Ephesians 1:3–6 says, "Praise be to the God and Father of our Lord Jesus Christ, who has blessed us in the heavenly realms with every spiritual blessing in Christ. For he chose us in him before the creation of the world to be holy and blameless in his sight. In love he predestined us to be adopted as his sons through Jesus Christ, in accordance with his pleasure and will—to the praise of his glorious grace, which he has freely given us in the One he loves." What does it really mean to be adopted as his sons? How can we show people not only what Jesus saves us from, but what he made it possible for us to become?

4. What is the difference between what we get from God and who we become in God? We not only have a choice to receive salvation, but also to allow Jesus to work in us and change us into his image. Why are there so many Christians who choose to keep living in their sin, much as they did before they were saved?

5. Why is mercy not enough to change the average man? How does the complete work of God's grace compare to mercy? How should we live our lives as adopted sons and heirs with Christ? Why are we required to share in his suffering? (See Romans 8:12–17.) As sons of God, what promises are ours for today? (John 10:10)

CHAPTER EIGHTEEN
THE POWER OF SIMPLY BEING PRESENT

1. Has the church in America lost sight of the individual? Why do you think that is or is not true of the church today?

2. Has a secular emphasis on success influenced how we run our church organizations? Do we somehow feel the need to justify the church's legitimacy by proving we can draw as many people to our events as other groups can?

3. What example did Jesus demonstrate in his ministry on earth? Crowds of people followed Jesus everywhere he went. He even managed to feed five thousand hungry men on a handful of fish and bread! (Matthew 4:23–25; Mark 6:30–44) Was he more interested in feeding the multitude or changing lives one person at a time—or both? What does this reveal about what our priorities should be?

4. Is there ever an appropriate time for a crowd mentality? How did the disciples manage when thousands of people accepted Christ at one time in the book of Acts? (Acts 2:14, 38–41) This phenomenon still happens today in evangelistic meetings and crusades around the world, where thousands upon thousands commit their lives to Christ in one service. Obviously, no individual minister can prepare for such overwhelming logistics. What role does the Holy Spirit play in bringing conviction and repentance, and guarding the hearts and faith of these new Christians?

5. Why are people often more attracted to a bar than a church? Remember the theme song to the sitcom *Cheers?* "Sometimes you want to go where everybody knows your name. And they're always glad you came." How does this

summarize what people wish they could experience in the body of Christ? In what ways does the individual fall through the cracks in our churches today? What can we do to be present and available so these situations do not happen?

CHAPTER NINETEEN
APOLOGETICS PROBLEM: NO ONE IS EVER ARGUED INTO THE KINGDOM

1. What is the definition of apologetics? Do you agree that apologetics should not be used primarily as a witnessing tool but to increase the faith of the believer? Why or why not?

2. Who or what is God's preferred form of communication? (Hebrews 1:1–2) Why does he sometimes use other methods to accomplish his will? Does the fact that some people may respond to apologetic arguments mean that they are the best—or wisest—approach? Should we assume that any and all methods are equally effective—even the use of donkeys?

3. How should we respond to people who are searching for meaning in their lives? Are statistics and reasoning the most effective tools to reach the lost? Why would people rather hear our own personal story? Why do we often feel it necessary to justify our experiences in order to prove the truth? Is it really possible to prove faith? (See Hebrews 11:1–3.)

4. When praying for the believers, Jesus said, "Righteous Father, though the world does not know you, I know you, and they know that you have sent me. I have made you known to them, and will continue to make you known in order that the love you have for me may be in them and that

I myself may be in them" (John 17:25–26). How does Christ make us known to the Father? How is relationship the key defining factor of our faith? Why is a personal encounter with Christ infinitely more powerful than logic?

5. All forms of argument—between friends, spouses, political opponents—inevitably boil down to one thing: offense. Whether we debate with quiet intensity or loud, vitriolic insults, all arguments end up the same way. Why is this a completely ineffective method to communicate the love of Jesus? Is there a point when an open, honest discussion can cross an invisible line and become an argument? Why will you never argue anyone into heaven?

CHAPTER TWENTY
DEVELOPING YOUR EVANGELISM STRATEGY

1. Do you have a personal evangelism strategy? If not, do you think the evangelism strategy described in this chapter is a reasonable and attainable goal for you? How can you implement these concepts into your daily life? Why is it important to write your plan down?

2. Are all salvation stories of equal power and merit? What is the potential danger of "country/western song" type testimonies? What great benefit can be gained from mature believers who have experienced both the peaks and the valleys of life, and who have survived to tell about it?

3. What is the hidden power of your own story? Do you sometimes feel you don't have anything important to say? Do you believe your testimony is insignificant compared to more glamorous or glorious tales of salvation? How can people be

changed by hearing about the personal trials and unique circumstances that led you to Christ?

4. What wisdom does Colossians 4:2–6 offer us as evangelists and servants of Jesus? How can we be ready and willing to season every conversation with salt and light?

The Word at Work Around the World

A vital part of Cook Communications Ministries is our international outreach, Cook Communications Ministries International (CCMI). Your purchase of this book, and of other books and Christian-growth products from Cook, enables CCMI to provide Bibles and Christian literature to people in more than 150 languages in 65 countries.

Cook Communications Ministries is a not-for-profit, self-supporting organization. Revenues from sales of our books, Bible curricula, and other church and home products not only fund our U.S. ministry, but also fund our CCMI ministry around the world. One hundred percent of donations to CCMI go to our international literature programs.

CCMI reaches out internationally in three ways:

· Our premier International Christian Publishing Institute (ICPI) trains leaders from nationally led publishing houses around the world.

· We provide literature for pastors, evangelists, and Christian workers in their national language.

· We reach people at risk—refugees, AIDS victims, street children, and famine victims—with God's Word.

Word Power, God's Power

Faith Kidz, RiverOak, Honor, Life Journey, Victor, NexGen — every time you purchase a book produced by Cook Communications Ministries, you not only meet a vital personal need in your life or in the life of someone you love, but you're also a part of ministering to José in Colombia, Humberto in Chile, Gousa in India, or Lidiane in Brazil. You help make it possible for a pastor in China, a child in Peru, or a mother in West Africa to enjoy a life-changing book. And because you helped, children and adults around the world are learning God's Word and walking in his ways.

Thank you for your partnership in helping to disciple the world. May God bless you with the power of his Word in your life.

For more information about our international ministries, visit www.ccmi.org.

Additional copies of *SPIRITUAL CPR*
and other NexGen titles are available
from your local bookseller.

◆ ◊ ◆

If you have enjoyed this book,
or if it has had an impact on your life,
we would like to hear from you.

Please contact us at:

NEXGEN BOOKS
Cook Communications Ministries, Dept. 201
4050 Lee Vance View
Colorado Springs, CO 80918
Or visit our Web site: www.cookministries.com

NEXGEN®

Building the New Generation of Believers